The Science Behind the
Art of Legal Writing

The Science Behind the Art of Legal Writing

Catherine J. Cameron

Lance N. Long

CAROLINA ACADEMIC PRESS

Durham, North Carolina

Library of Congress Cataloging-in-Publication Data

Cameron, Catherine J., author.
 The science behind the art of legal writing / Catherine J. Cameron and Lance N. Long.
    pages cm
 Includes bibliographical references and index.
 ISBN 978-1-61163-014-5 (alk. paper)
 1. Legal composition. 2. Legal research. 3. Law--Language. I. Long, Lance N., author. II. Title.

 K94.C33 2014
 808.06'634--dc23

                         2014032801

Carolina Academic Press
700 Kent Street
Durham, North Carolina 27701
Telephone (919) 489-7486
Fax (919) 493-5668
www.cap-press.com

Printed in the United States of America

To Brett and Amy

Contents

Acknowledgments

We thank our wonderful research assistants Adam LaBonte, Chantel Green, Kara Large, Kristen O'Donnell, Elise Pautler, Giovanni Giarratana, and the many other research assistants who have helped us in our previous studies cited in this book. We also thank our colleagues who have worked with us on previous articles and studies discussed in this book, particularly William Christensen. We could (would?) not have written this book without the generous support of Stetson University College of Law, and we thank the administration for its support of our scholarship and this book. Finally, we thank Amy Oaks Long for her editing and proofreading over the entire course of writing this book.

The Science Behind the Art
of Legal Writing

Introduction

"And now for something completely different."

Monty Python

There are more than 150 books on legal writing in the known universe[1] and virtually all of them give this directive to budding legal writers—a legal writer should keep the use of intensifiers to a minimum. Many of these books point to the fact that words like "clearly," "obviously," and "really" are superfluous at best. If an argument is clear or obvious, the reader will know from reading the argument. Highlighting the clarity or obviousness with an intensifier, therefore, conveys no meaning beyond what the reader has already gleaned from the excellent legal prose before him or her. More Orwellian legal writing textbooks indicate that intensifiers highlight writers' insecurities in the quality of their arguments, and readers, not unlike horses, are quick to sense insecurities. The theory goes that once the reader senses these insecurities the entire argument is undermined.

This dislike for intensifiers is not reserved for authors of legal writing texts. The Chief Justice of the Supreme Court holds intensifiers in disdain as well. In a speech to Northwestern Law School, Chief Justice Roberts said,

> We get hundreds and hundreds of briefs, and they're all the same.... Somebody says, "My client clearly deserves to win, the cases clearly do this, the language clearly reads this," blah, blah, blah. And you pick up the other side and, lo and behold, they think they clearly deserve to win. How about a little recognition that it's a tough job? ... I mean if it was an easy case, we wouldn't have it.[2]

---

1. This number was calculated by running a search for "legal writing" in the Amazon.com Books database.

2. Robert Barnes, *Chief Justice Counsels Humility: Roberts Says Lawyers Must Put Themselves in Judges' Shoes*, WASH. POST, Feb. 6, 2007, at A15.

Chief Justice Roberts is not alone among his robed colleagues. There have been several surveys of judges, which have discovered that a certain subset of judges— at least, those judges lucky enough to be presiding over a California or Utah jurisdiction—found reading superfluous intensifiers onerous.[3]

As many legal writers before us have no doubt wondered, we wondered, what is so "bad" about intensifiers that virtually all of the authorities on the subject of legal writing vilify their use? Is the use of intensifiers in a brief a recipe for a failed legal argument? Does the use of intensifiers undermine the persuasiveness of an argument? Are intensifiers so distracting to a judge that the judge no longer pays attention or gives any credit to a legal argument? Or might an intensifier-rich brief be more persuasive or more clear for a legal reader even if judges don't particularly like reading intensifiers?

Unfortunately, we could not find the answers to most of our questions in any single legal writing textbook, so we began to look for some empirical support for the anti-intensifier movement on our own. We looked through legal writing textbooks. We questioned authors. We questioned publishers. We scoured law reviews and academic research journals, but nowhere could we find any sort of study that had been conducted to find out if the use of intensifiers diminishes the effectiveness of a legal argument.

So, one of us decided to conduct his own study. That study showed that intensifiers are not necessarily "bad." The study assessed 800 briefs from 400 randomly selected state and federal cases. Although the study showed a correlation between losing an appeal and a high level of intensifier use in a brief written by the losing party in the case, the study also discovered that briefs with a high level of intensifiers fared better if the judge also used a high level of intensifiers in his or her opinion of the case, suggesting that intensifiers are either persuasive in some instances or that the negative effects of those intensifiers did not cause the judge to rule against the party using them. Some legal writing textbook authors may find support in this study for their dislike of intensifiers, but a close read of it indicates that there may be some times when intensifier use can be effective, and it is likely an overstatement to say that the occasional use of an intensifier will cause a party to lose a case.

Although limiting intensifier use is a relatively insignificant maxim of legal writing, other maxims and conventions are more significant, and yet there is generally little discussion of the empirical bases for these important maxims and conventions. For example, some legal writers ascribe to the belief that organizational schemes such as "CRAC" (Conclusion-Rule-Analysis-Conclusion)

---

3. Lance N. Long & William F. Christensen, *Clearly, Using Intensifiers is Bad—or is It?*, 45 Idaho L. R. 171, 175–76 (2008).

or "IRAC" (Issue-Rule-Analysis-Conclusion) are better than other organizational formats, but is there any empirical evidence that these schemes are better than other schemes? Other legal writers insist on starting every document with a preview of the conclusion of the document, but do legal readers really need a conclusion at the beginning of a document to best understand the legal argument that follows?

Another significant legal writing convention regards the use of "plain language." Does it really make a difference whether shorter sentences, shorter words, and active voice are used? Maybe plain language actually reduces the semantic flow of complex arguments, making them more difficult to understand.

The problem of determining whether something "works" in the practice of legal writing, and finding some rational basis for making the claim that something "works" also applies to how we teach or learn legal writing. In the words of one who specializes in learning psychology: "We have known [certain empirically established principles of learning] for some time, and it's intriguing that schools don't pick them up, or that people don't learn them by trial and error[.] ... Instead, we walk around with all sorts of unexamined beliefs about what works that are mistaken."[4]

If you are reading this book as part of your first year of law school, you may be surprised to learn that "legal writing" as a required part of the first year curriculum is a relatively recent phenomenon in law schools across the United States. Before the 1960s, legal writing was taught in a haphazard fashion. Most schools had some sort of "legal bibliography" course that taught students how to conduct legal research, and some schools had courses that sought to teach students basic grammar and writing structure, generally staffed by graduate students. But in the 1960s, a movement began to study and teach legal writing as a true academic discipline in law schools by full-time law professors with a strong focus on the description of legal authority and logical application of that legal authority to the facts that support a well-written legal analysis.[5]

Every law school in the country now has a writing program geared towards teaching the skills students need to analyze and present the law to courts, other attorneys and clients. And while there are plenty of textbooks that have been

---

4. Benedict Carey, *Forget What you Know About Good Study Habits*, http://www.ny-times.com/2010/09/07/health/views/07mind.html?pagewanted=all (last modified Sept. 8, 2010).

5. Margorie Dick Rombauer is credited as the founder of legal writing as an academic discipline in law schools. Margorie taught at the University of Washington and was the first to create a legal writing teaching program and to write a textbook supporting that program. An Interview with Margorie Rumbauer, 20 The Journal of the Legal Writing Institute 19 (2003).

written over the years to compliment the legal writing classroom, we believe this is the first book that has compiled the empirical basis for so many of the directives legal writing teachers and legal writing textbooks give students about legal writing.

This book is a single source for learning and understanding the theoretical and empirical bases for legal writing and seeks to arm the novice legal writer with empirical knowledge so that the writer can make logical and informed choices about how to structure legal writing. Although writing is an "art" in many senses of the word, there is some "science" behind the "art" of legal writing, and that "science" is what this book explains. This book will highlight the numerous studies performed in various academic fields on the viability and efficacy of writing choices and will demonstrate how those studies support or criticize choices when it comes to legal writing.

While we hesitate to say that there are "rights" and "wrongs" to legal writing like there are to mathematical equations, there are various writing choices that will almost always cause a reader difficulty comprehending the writer's message. There are some writing choices that have no clear "right" or "wrong" and are simply the "art" part of legal writing. The only way to know how to make good "artistic" choices in those instances is to survey legal readers to see what choices are supported by a majority of readers. Many such polls have been taken, and we discuss the results of those polls in this book as well. To help you assess those sorts of "artistic" choices, we include exercises at the end of appropriate chapters that give you a chance to separate the writing choices that are supported by empirical science from those that are simply preferences and deserve a more "artistic" approach. Then, you can use these samples to consider which "artistic" choices are preferable through discussions with your peers and your professors. In the end, we hope you feel empowered to take the information from this book and apply it to whatever legal writing challenges you face in the future.

PART I
Science and Writing

Chapter 1

Why Apply Science to Writing?

The answer to the question posed by the chapter title may be answered with the same philosophical flippancy evinced by the answer to the question "Why does one climb the mountain?" The answer to both questions is "Because it is there." Seriously, science is a method that is recognized by most educated people as a valid means for proving hypotheses. The scientific method is used in many disciplines and is generally believed to maintain the integrity of the disciplines. Four components uphold that integrity: "(1) repeatability, (2) open communication (data sharing), (3) objective interpretation (statistical inference), and (4) peer review."[1] In order for the scientific method to work, however, variables must be controlled, and devising and conducting scientific tests on legal writing is particularly problematic because controlling the myriad of variables on the part of both the writer and reader is difficult. (Trust us, we have done scientific and statistical legal writing studies, and it is painstaking and time-consuming.)

Nevertheless, an immense amount of scientific research has been done on writing in general, and much of it is applicable to legal writing. Unfortunately, much less research has been done specifically with legal writing (most likely because the legal field has been relatively short sighted and has only recently embraced the value of cross-disciplinary collaboration and research). Kathryn Stanchi accurately summarizes the situation:

> Instead, the study of persuasive writing has been dominated by a kind of "armchair psychology"—a set of conventions and practices, handed down from lawyer to lawyer, developed largely from instinct and speculation. By and large, the information available to students and lawyers about persuasive legal writing reproduces these conventions and practices without analysis or critique, and without taking stock of the growing body of research from other disciplines that would provide

---

1. Katherine L. Gross & Gary G. Mittelbach, *What Maintains the Integrity of Science: An Essay for Nonscientists*, 58 Emory L.J. 341, 342 (2008–2009).

some evidence about whether the conventional wisdom is an accurate account of human decision making.[2]

The few studies specific to legal writing include surveys of judges and attorneys to assess writing preferences; simulated studies using students, judges, practitioners, and lay people; and scientific and statistical analyses of actual legal writing.

In a similar vein, what has been said by Michael J. Saks with respect to the teaching of trial advocacy and practice is also true of the teaching of legal writing. Saks argues that these programs suffer from reliance on intuition and tradition rather than empirical verification:

> Effective answers about 'what works' will not come from reflection or intuition but from empirical inquiries: from concrete experience, from experimental tests of alternative techniques, and perhaps from borrowing findings about phenomena of persuasion from disciplines that study persuasion empirically. Things are changing, however, and in the last twenty years much more empirical analysis and scientific testing specifically directed towards legal writing has been done to test the long-held beliefs of legal writers and legal writing teachers in general.[3]

Asked to answer whether there were any empirical studies showing that the quality of legal writing can help a lawyer win a case or an appeal, Wayne Schiess answered that "in general, the answer is no—there are few studies on that question. But new research is occurring...." Schiess points to two studies performed by Professors Lance N. Long and William F. Christensen, as well as a third study performed by Sean Flammer, all of which are discussed in this book.[4]

This book examines various aspects of legal writing, and each chapter addresses a specific topic. All the chapters follow the same basic format. First,

---

2. Kathryn M. Stanchi, *The Science of Persuasion: An Initial Exploration*, 2006 MICH. ST. L. REV. 1, 2.

3. Michael J. Saks, *Turning Practice into Progress: Better Lawyering Through Experimentation*, 66 NOTRE DAME L. REV. 801, 802 (1990–1991).

4. Wayne Schiess, *Research on Persuasive Legal Writing*, AUSTIN LAWYER MAGAZINE, March 2011, at 1, citing the following three studies: Lance N. Long & William F. Christensen, *Clearly, Using Intensifiers Is Very Bad—Or Is It?* 45 Idaho L. Rev. 171 (2008); Lance N. Long & William F. Christensen, *Does the Readability of Your Brief Affect Your Chance of Winning an Appeal?—An Analysis of Readability in Appellate Briefs and Its Correlation with Success on Appeal*, 12 J. App. Prac. & Proc. 145 (2011); Sean Flammer, *Persuading Judges: An Empirical Analysis of Writing Style, Persuasion, and the Use of Plain English*, 16 Legal Writing 184 (2010).

the particular legal writing topic is explained. Second, treatment of the subject by other legal writing textbooks is discussed. Third, the relevant scientific and/or statistical research (or the lack of relevant scientific and/or statistical research) is discussed, and finally, the bottom line—what the research means—for law students, lawyers, and legal writers in general is discussed.

It is our hope that this book will provide an informative introduction to the science of legal writing and helpful information for all legal writers.

Chapter 2

Some Caveats on Science Applied to Writing

"Science is not immune to lying and cheating, any more than are banking, medicine, or the law."[1]

While there is a paucity of empirical support for legal practice, and particularly, for legal writing, science does not guarantee better answers to legal writing questions because science has its own foibles. Recently, the spotlight has shown on several leading scholars whose published scientific research has been retracted because of fraud.[2] The culprits aren't limited to any one particular discipline; they come from medicine,[3] psychology,[4] physics,[5] chemistry,[6] and other disciplines.[7] While fraud is not new and there are examples of leading authorities committing research fraud dating back decades, more attention has been

---

1. Alan Kraut, *Despite Occasional Scandals, Science Can Police Itself*, CHRON. HIGHER EDUC., Dec. 9, 2011, at A72.

2. Trends E-Mag., *Dealing with Scientific Fraud*, TRENDS E-MAG., http://www.audiotech.com/trends-magazine/dealing-with-scientific-fraud/ (June 2013).

3. Olle ten Cate et al, *Research Fraud and Its Combat: What Can a Journal Do?*, 47 MED. EDUC. 638–640 (2013).

4. Matthew C. Makel, Jonathan A. Plucker & Boyd Hegarty, *Replications in Psychology Research: How Often Do They Really Occur?* 7 PERSP. ON PSYCHOL. SCI. 537 (2012).

5. *See* Eugenie Samuel Reich, *Plastic Fantastic: How the Biggest Fraud in Physics Shook the Scientific World* (2010).

6. Bill Frezza, *A Barrage Of Legal Threats Shuts Down Whistleblower Site*, FORBES (Jan. 9, 2013), www.forbes.com/sites/billfrezza/2013/01/09/a-barrage-of-legal-threats-shuts-down-whistleblower-site-science-fraud/print/.

7. See Andrew Gelman & Thomas Basboll, *To Throw Away Data: Plagiarism as a Statistical Crime*, 101 AM. SCI. 168 (May-June 2013) (statistics); Kálmán Abari, *Reproducible Research in Speech Sciences*, INT'L J. COMPUTER SCI. ISSUES, Nov. 2012, at 43 (speech); James E. Kennedy, *Experimenter Misconduct in Parapsychology: Analysis Manipulation and Fraud* (May 21, 2013), http://jeksite.org/psi/misconduct.pdf (parapsychology).

recently placed on rooting out fraudulent studies and implementing safeguards to prevent, or at least limit, further publication of fraudulent articles. The reasons for committing research fraud are diverse: pressure on academics to publish in order to get jobs or promotions or tenure, difficulty in achieving the desired results in a study, the ease of getting away with it from understaffed journals who are unable to catch the fraud, or psychological issues that make a fraudster's motives difficult to ascertain. Regardless of the reason for the fraud, the costs of such fraud are enormous—millions of dollars in grant funds spent on research that is essentially worthless, dark shadows cast over the careers of students who work under or in conjunction with fraudsters that might lead to their own research and publications being questioned, retractions of articles and studies that are cited in other studies that lead to questions of the methods used in honestly conducted studies, lives at risk for fraudulent medical and psychological studies that doctors rely on when treating patients, and doubts cast on entire disciplines and academia as a whole.

While many of the instances of discovered fraud have failed to include one of the four critical components necessary to maintain integrity—(1) repeatability, (2) open communication (data sharing), (3) objective interpretation (statistical inference), and (4) peer review analysis—it is often difficult for a reader of a scientific article to know that one or more of the components is missing. It is for this reason that fraud in the sciences undermines the scientific community as a whole.

Research fraud can come in all shapes and sizes. In addition to the kind of issues that might arise in any form of scholarship, like plagiarism, conflicts of interest, and ethical issues, there are unique ways for an author of an empirical analysis to commit fraud: fabricating data, omission of data, invalid procedures for handling data, data-snooping, cherry-picking, and harking.[8]

One example that has sparked widespread attention to academic fraud and raised the call for more safeguards to prevent further fraud is that of Diederik Stapel, who was called "The Lying Dutchman" by *The Washington Post*.[9] Stapel, a Dutch

---

8. René Bekkers, *Risk factors for fraud and academic misconduct in the social sciences* (Nov. 29, 2012, 2:29 PM), http://renebekkers.wordpress.com/2012/11/29/risk-factors-for-fraud-and-academic-misconduct-in-the-social-sciences/. Data snooping is when a study is completed before target sample is achieved because the desired result is achieved. Cherry picking is when data is not reported because it does not support the hypothesis. Harking is when the hypothesis is created after the results of the data are known. *Id.*

9. Joel Achenbach, *Diederik Stapel: The Lying Dutchman*, WASHINGTON POST (Nov. 1, 2011, 5:38 PM), http://www.washingtonpost.com/blogs/achenblog/post/diederik-stapel-the-lying-dutchman/2011/11/01/gIQA86XOdM_blog.html.

psychologist who became dean of the School of Social and Behavioral Sciences at Tilburg University in the Netherlands, published over thirty studies in which he admitted to completely fabricating the data used to achieve his desired results.[10] His articles "on the effect of power on hypocrisy, on racial stereotyping and on how advertisements affect how people view themselves"[11] were published in many journals, cited by numerous media outlets and scholarly articles, and launched him to become a highly regarded "academic star" around the world.[12] In an interview, Stapel "described his behavior as an addiction that drove him to carry out acts of increasingly daring fraud, like a junkie seeking a bigger and better high."[13]

Stapel's fraud was discovered by students at his school who found "anomalies" in the data of his research.[14] In many of his studies, Stapel had created his own data to create the result he desired for writing his paper. Although some were suspicious of Stapel's work, it was hard for them to prove his fraud because he kept most of his data to himself and, when it was requested by others, Stapel would often not be able to provide it. Suspicions were also raised because the data that Stapel used in his studies were "amazing data sets."[15] Ultimately, Stapel admitted to his fraud, forfeited his Ph.D. and his position, and many of his articles were retracted—and those that were not retracted will be viewed with doubt in the future.

In addition to the consequences faced by Stapel, many others—possibly the whole psychology field—face consequences and skepticism. Stapel's actions have led many journals across various disciplines to set up further safeguards in their publication process.

Another area of psychology that has been subject to much criticism, and increased scrutiny, is "behavioral or goal priming, research that demonstrates how subliminal prompts can make you do all manner of crazy things."[16] Professor John Bargh has received much scrutiny on his studies in the last few years,

---

10. Yudhijit Bhattacharjee, *The Mind of a Con Man*, N.Y. Times Mag. (Apr. 26, 2013), http://www.nytimes.com/2013/04/28/magazine/diederik-stapels-audacious-academic-fraud.html?pagewanted=all&_r=0.

11. Benedict Carey, *Fraud Case Seen as a Red Flag for Psychology Research*, N.Y. TIMES (Nov. 2, 2011), http://www.nytimes.com/2011/11/03/health/research/noted-dutch-psychologist-stapel-accused-of-research-fraud.html?_r=3.

12. Bhattacharjee, *supra* n. 10.

13. *Id.*

14. *Id.*

15. *Id.*

16. Tom Bartlett, *Power of Suggestion*, CHRON. HIGHER EDUC. (Jan. 30, 2013), http://chronicle.com/article/Power-of-Suggestion/136907/.

scrutiny which has been widely cited and increased his reputation in academia.[17] Much of the scrutiny is the result of other academics who are skeptical of his research, because they tried to replicate his published studies and had a difficult time obtaining the same results.[18] Because the results of his studies yielded controversial conclusions,[19] it led other academics to examine how the results were reached. While the unsuccessful attempts at replication haven't led to the article retractions and career-ending consequences suffered by Professor Stapel, Professor Bargh's reputation has been challenged.

While it is up to the scientific community as a whole to police scientific analysis for fraud, two resources for those looking to learn more about fraud are Retraction Watch,[20] and the Office of Research Integrity in the United States Department of Health and Human Services.[21]

Psychologists are not the only academics suffering from accusations of fraud; historians have also been accused of fraud and dishonesty. Often, the work of academics is subject to more scrutiny when their work is controversial or challenges beliefs held dear by particular political groups. For example, Michael Bellesiles wrote a book entitled *Arming America* that came under attack by groups like the National Rifle Association.[22] While some of his conclusions were the result of "inadequate documentation" and "interpretation,"[23] Bellesiles' reputation and career were severely damaged because of the pressures put on him.[24]

While the NRA attacked Bellesiles' work, it strongly supported the work of John Lott Jr.'s book, *More Guns, Less Crime*, which has led some states to "pass what are called 'concealed carry' gun laws" as a result of the book's conclusions

---

17. "Priming is what Bargh is known for. When he says 'my name is a symbol that stands for these kinds of effects,' he's not being arrogant. That's a fact." *Id.*

18. *Id.*

19. Professor Bargh's first controversial experiment concluded that certain words on a page (words like "bingo" and "Florida," "knits" and "wrinkles," "bitter" and "alone") could trigger a person to act old. *Id.* "One ... experiment[ ] tested subjects to see if they were more hostile when primed with an African-American face. They were. (The subjects were not African-American.) In [another] experiment, the subjects were primed with rude words to see if that would make them more likely to interrupt a conversation. It did." *Id.*

20. RETRACTION WATCH, http://retractionwatch.wordpress.com/ (last visited Aug. 25, 2013).

21. OFFICE OF RESEARCH INTEGRITY, http://ori.dhhs.gov/ (last visited Aug. 25, 2013).

22. Jon Wiener, *Historians in Trouble: Plagiarism, Fraud and Politics in the Ivory Tower* 76, New Press (2007).

23. *Id.* at 74.

24. Bellesiles was subject to much scrutiny and committees were formed to check his work. Ultimately, Bellesiles quit his professorship at Emory University because of the pressure placed on him by his critics. *Id.*

that "evidence show[s] that states that permit citizens to carry guns have lower crime rates."[25] However, the statistics provided by Lott did not seem correct, and many critics questioned his findings. Lott provided different excuses for his results—first saying his finding that "98 percent of the time that people use guns defensively, they merely have to brandish a weapon to break off an attack"[26] came from other studies and then saying that the figure came from a national survey he personally conducted. However, when asked for the data, Lott said it was lost to a computer crash.[27] Interestingly, Lott's career did not suffer as a result of the scrutiny he received to the same extent that Michael Bellesiles' career did.[28]

The important thing for readers of this book to remember is that the studies discussed in the following chapters may not be as reliable as we might hope them to be. This is particularly true of the "priming" studies that have been cited by many legal writing scholars as a basis for putting important emotional information at the beginning of a persuasive legal memo. We cite to some priming-type studies and many other types of studies that may be similar to other studies that have been discredited, but we have not knowingly discussed any discredited study. And although some empirical studies have been discredited over the years, we believe that the many that remain valid can teach us much about making informed choices for our legal writing.

---

25. *Id.* at 136.

26. *Id.* at 137 (quoting Jon R. Lott, Jr., MORE GUNS, LESS CRIME 3 (1998)).

27. *Id.* at 139. This is in addition to the fact that he could provide no records—telephone bills, survey sheets, or names of students who had worked with him on the survey.

28. *Id.* at 148.

PART II
Before You Start Writing

Chapter 3

A Word About Legal Research and Outlining

There are many textbooks that detail the intricacies of legal research for a new law student, and those details are beyond the confines of this textbook. However, the intersection between legal research and the legal writing project is an important consideration for new legal writers. Many textbooks counsel new legal writers to be sure to complete the research project prior to embarking on the written project. These same textbooks often have a chapter devoted to outlining, a process that requires a legal writer to understand fully the issues the legal writer wants to cover in the writing project in order to make organizational choices for the outline. Legal writing places a heavy emphasis on building analysis on existing legal authority—statutes, case law, and the like. Judges pay very little attention to arguments that are not built on legal authority. Therefore, in order to fully understand the analysis that a writer will be describing to a reader, the writer must have completed all research prior to outlining.

Although there is no empirical research that specifically looks at the intersection between legal research and legal writing, there is much research in the area of cognitive psychology that looks at the process of writing and whether a writer needs to completely understand what the writer plans to communicate prior to putting pen to paper or if the writer can write an effective composition by learning during the writing process. Like so much of the research that we look at in this book, the results are a bit mixed, and a new legal writer may very well find that the best plan of action is a bit of self-assessment in order to determine whether the writer should complete all legal research before writing. And sometimes, the practicalities of the writing project make the decision for the writer. If you don't discover the need to research an issue until after you begin writing, there is no way around the fact that you will have to retro-fit that research in to any existing outline or writing you have completed, which may not have been what you would have done if you had known of the issue prior to beginning your writing process.

One of the most prolific researchers in the area of cognitive psychology and the writing process is Ronald Kellogg. In the late 1980s and early 1990s Kellogg conducted a series of studies that looked at college students and their writing process. In one study Kellogg took 207 college students and gave them prompts from essays required for the Law School Admissions Test because these essays required a significant amount of analysis.[1] Kellogg gave one group of students a suggested organizational strategy for the essay and suggested topics to cover, he gave another group of students suggested topics to cover only and no suggested organizational outline, and he gave another group of students no further instructions beyond the essay prompt.

Kellogg then took each of these three groups and instructed half of them on the art of linear outlining, that is, creating a detailed outline of the progression of the paper from beginning to end that indicates the specific order in which material will be covered. He instructed the other half of each group on cluster outlining, that is, a non-linear outlining process that asked students to simply list terms that describe various ideas on a piece of paper and draw lines between ideas that have connections to each other.

Kellogg then had two judges assess the quality of the essays, and he discovered that outlining in a linear form did create a better style and content of essay than not outlining or using the non-linear form of outlining for all of the students except the ones that were given a detailed outline to follow and the topics to cover before beginning the essay. Those students that were given a detailed outline to follow and topics to cover before beginning the essay did not seem to benefit in any significant way from conducting their own outlining process before starting to write their essay.

Kellogg also noted that the students appeared to write the essay faster if they had prepared a linear outline before beginning the writing process or had the outline given to them, a finding that was especially significant for those students who developed their own linear outline. He attributed this increase in speed, along with the increased style quality of the essay to an efficient use of attention and working memory. Because a writer is only able to devote a finite amount of attention and working memory to a task, planning the organization and topics to be covered prior to writing takes those tasks off the plate of the writer and allows the writer to focus on drafting coherent sentences that effectively communicate the ideas at hand.

Despite the support this study seemed to give for the linear outlining process, Kellogg did note that his study did not look at writers dealing with writers block, who he pointed out had been shown in a previous study to be the kind of writers that use the outlining process as a means of procrastination. Con-

---

1. Ronald T. Kellogg, *Effectiveness of Prewriting Strategies as a Function of Task Demands*, 103 AM. J. OF PSYCHOL., 327–342 (1990).

sequently, it may be beneficial for writers with writer's block to begin writing without outlining first.

The applications of Kellogg's study for a legal writer are largely affected by the individual nature of the legal writer and the specific legal writing project. If a legal writer is writing a document that involves a form the legal writer has written in before, or a topic the writer is familiar with, outlining may have little effect on the quality of the end product and may be a waste of time. If the legal writer is given a form to follow but the content of the writing is new to the legal writer, creating a linear outline before writing may have some benefit to the quality of the end product, but that benefit is not as clear as when a writer is embarking on a project where the writer does not have a specific organizational form to follow and is dealing with a topic area that the writer has not dealt with before. It is in those situations that a writer can benefit from reducing the attention and working memory load during the writing process by creating a linear outline ahead of time that allows the writer to fully form an organizational strategy and the connections between ideas before embarking on the writing process.

Most new legal writers would find themselves in the category of someone that would benefit from a linear outline in most instances. However, Kellogg's note about writer's block is an important one to consider. If you are someone who finds that creating an outline seems to take an enormous amount of time, you may actually be using the outlining process as a means of procrastination, which is obviously counterproductive to the writing process. Those writers who find that outlining before they begin writing is largely a procrastination tool may find the process of reverse outlining to be more effective. Reverse outlining involves taking a written document and reducing it to an outline form to access the connections in the analysis in a more simplistic fashion. It follows that assessing your progress on a writing project if you do choose to outline is important to determine if outlining is worth the effort.

If it is determined that creating a linear outline is beneficial for your writing project, then completing your legal research first is a necessity. It is hard to imagine how a writer would create a linear outline that organizes analysis without fully understanding that analysis. And since legal analysis is built on legal authority it follows that the writer must be knowledgeable of that legal authority before beginning the outline. However, there is one more important caveat that a novice legal writer should be aware of when deciding whether their legal research needs to be completed before beginning writing.

In the last few decades there have been many educational theorists who have discussed the benefits of learning through writing. Although there is not much empirical testing of these theories,[2] they seem to be well accepted at most of the higher education institutions in America. Based largely on the theories of Janet Emig,[3] a scholar in the field of education, these programs are built on the foundation that the unique nature of writing allows someone who is writing as they learn to have a concrete transcript of their thoughts that can be reviewed and evaluated. Emig also notes that the process of organizing writing often helps writers recognize conceptual groupings on a sheet of paper better than the writer would have noticed these groupings in their own minds.

These theories have some important implications for a novice legal writer. Even though it may be ideal to complete all legal research before beginning an outlining and writing process, sometimes it is either impractical because a writer will not understand certain connections between legal issues before beginning the writing process or because a writer may not understand the gaps in his or her knowledge until the writer begins the writing process.

Certainly, the practicalities of writing may give the legal writer no choice in the legal research process. If a legal writer discovers midway through writing a document that there is an issue that the writer failed to research, the writer will have no choice but to research the issue at that point and then to go back and retroactively fit the analysis of that issue into any outline or text the writer has drafted. However, it does appear that there is significant empirical evidence that demonstrates that if a novice legal writer can fully complete the research process before creating a linear outline, the final written product will, indeed, be a product of better quality both in style and content.

As with so many of the recommendations that come out of empirical research, it is important to remember that life does not always mimic controlled laboratory situations. Each individual writer must assess his or her own learning and writing tendencies and the aspects of the individual writing project that may necessitate research or outlining to be completed prior to writing a document. Armed with the knowledge of the empirical research that has been conducted in this area and the theories that support the benefits of learning through the writing process, a legal writer can make educated choices about legal research and outlining efforts and where this effort should fit into the writing process.

---

2. Most of the scholarship on the "Writing Across the Curriculum" movement is largely descriptive and anecdotal. See Patricia Kolb, Implementation of Writing Across the Curriculum (WAC) Learning Approaches in Social Work and Sociology Gerontology Courses, Gerontology & Geriatrics Education, 34:2, 212–223 (2013) (describing the guiding literature for the "Writing Across the Curriculum" movement).

3. Janet Emig, *Writing as a Mode of Learning*, COLLEGE COMPOSITION AND COMMUNICATION 122–128, (1977).

Outlining does not have to follow the traditional Roman numeral outlining structure you may have been taught in elementary school. Any pre-planning of your writing will accomplish, at least, some of the attributes seen in these empirical studies.

Outline Exercise

Let's try out an exercise that will help you determine if outlining will work for you.

Imagine you were asked to write a chapter for an elementary school textbook on the steps someone needs to take in order to successfully apply to law school. Use the space below or a separate piece of paper to create an outline or to simply write down thoughts about what you would want to cover in that chapter:

Now that you have finished your outlining process—whether it be a formal, Roman numeral linear outline, or an informal, free-flow of jotted-down ideas— turn those thoughts into a coherent text in this space or on a separate piece of paper:

Now, imagine you are going to take this explanation a step further and explain the steps involved in progressing through law school and becoming a barred attorney. This time, don't preplan your writing at all. Simply write what you would include in this explanation below or on a separate piece of paper:

Looking back at the portion of your chapter that explained the steps involved in getting to law school, compare that to the portion of your chapter that explained the steps involved in getting from law school to being a barred attorney. Are there any differences? Which section is better? Which section did you find easier to write? The answers to these questions will help you determine if outlining is a beneficial exercise for your mental processing of writing.

Chapter 4

Introduction to Legal Documents

"Legal writing" is a phrase that encompasses any sort of writing that describes the law and how the law applies to a particular set of facts. As you can imagine, this means that many types of documents involve legal writing. Most people think of traditional legal documents that are submitted to a court as legal writing—briefs, motions, and the like. However, there are a litany of documents that a lawyer may write on any given day involving legal analysis that are never submitted to a court. Transactional documents, such as contracts, wills, and leases, all involve legal analysis, even though sometimes that analysis is not expressed in the text of the document so much as it is used to determine the document's wording to effect the correct legal significance of the document. Additionally, lawyers are often called on to draft simple letters or e-mails to clients that explain the lawyer's legal analysis of the client's situation. There are even some lawyers that write academic articles, such as law review articles or bar journal articles that involve legal analysis.

One of the first things that you will have to do when embarking on a new legal writing project is to determine exactly what you need to produce at the end of the project. The following is a description of the main types of legal writing that you will come across in practice and the specific considerations you should take when embarking on these types of legal writing projects.

Client Communications, Legal Memos, and Other Inter-Office Communication Documents

Many first-year legal writing courses start with having students write an objective "office memo." Office memos were common communication devices prior to the Internet age. The office memo was a document that allowed law firms to create institutional memory. When lawyers researched a particular legal issue and wrote down their analysis in a memorandum format, it allowed that document to not only be mailed to a client, but then be filed in a manner that was retrievable by a lawyer looking at the same issue later on.

This system, in theory, allowed the subsequent lawyer to take advantage of the first lawyer's work product, thereby saving the firm time and the client money. Some large law firms still keep highly indexed banks of office memos and other legal documents. The need for quick searchability of these memos in paper form necessitated many formalities to the written products that may not be needed now that memos are largely in electronic format. Traditional legal memos often have headings that indicate who the memo is for, who the memo is from, the date of the memo and what the memo regards, issue statements that briefly summarize the legal issue addressed in the memo, brief answers that quickly answer the issue for the reader, a separately written facts section that details the important legal facts for the reader to understand, and a separately headed conclusion section that, generally, reiterates in greater detail the information in the brief answer. These sections, other than the main discussion of the legal analysis, allowed readers of paper documents to gain previews of the main document to decide if it was worth their time to read the full document.

Many of the reasons for formal legal memos are not relevant in the Internet age. Lawyers often communicate with clients by email, where there is no expectation for particular formatting because email tends to reformat itself to comport with the receiver's email system. Additionally, because of text searchability on most word processing programs, the need for the preview sections of formal memos is largely gone. If a subsequent lawyer wants to know if a document addresses a particular issue, the subsequent lawyer can simply search for that language in the document.

A survey conducted by a Georgetown University legal writing professor, of Georgetown alumni from classes dating back to 1983, demonstrated that the formal legal memo is no longer a widely used mode of communication in law firms.[1] Firms now have less formal systems of passing on knowledge to clients and from one lawyer to another through the use of email and informal memos— memos that have much less of the preview information of the traditional formal legal memo. The alumni that were surveyed, however, did note that there were rare occasions where they were asked to draft a formal legal memo, and the majority felt that teaching a formal traditional legal memo style is good practice in case a legal writer is ever called upon to draft such a formal memo. Additionally, the alumni felt that it is much easier for new lawyers to modify what

---

1. Kristen Konrad Robbins-Tiscione, *From Snail Mail to E-Mail: The Traditional Legal Memorandum in the Twenty-First Century*, 58 J. LEGAL EDUC. 32–60 (2008).

they know about writing a traditional legal memo to less formal styles, like an informal memo or an email, instead of having to learn about parts of a traditional legal memo once in practice.

Although a legal writing professor may decide that it is more meaningful for a student to learn a writing format for communication with clients and other lawyers that is more like the format that a new graduate will likely face, it is important for students to know the history of the traditional legal memo and the specific preview parts of a legal memo just in case the student is ever called upon to draft something similar.

Most formal legal memos call for an objective writing tone, in that they are usually assessments of the law that are not designed to persuade as much as to inform.

For instance, when a client asks a lawyer for information, or when a senior lawyer in a firm asks a junior lawyer to assess a legal issue, those recipients are looking for an objective legal analysis. In other words, an explanation of the law and how that law applies to the facts that is frank and honest about the likely outcome of the situation if a court is ever to look at the issue. And even though a less formal legal memo or e-mail may contain less of the preview components of a traditional legal memo (headings, issue statements, brief answers, statements of facts, or conclusions), any legal analysis, no matter how informal, contains what a traditional legal memo would label as a "Discussion" section, which is the section where the lawyer describes the law and how the law applies to the facts at hand.

Communications with Opposing Parties, Briefs, and Other Litigation Documents

After a lawyer assesses a legal issue from an objective standpoint, the lawyer can then move to looking at the issue from a persuasive standpoint, that is, a standpoint where the lawyer presents the law and the application of the law to a reader in a manner that makes that legal analysis as beneficial for the client's position as possible. Because many persuasive documents are submitted to courts, there are often particularized requirements imposed by a receiving court. These requirements can include everything from the types of information that the court wants in specifically labeled sections of the document to formatting requirements, like font size and page limits. Many court rules follow the Federal Rules of Appellate Procedure, which require the following sections of a brief: a table of contents that identifies the page number where each section begins in the brief, a table of authorities that indicates the page numbers where readers can find all authorities cited in the brief, a statement of jurisdiction that indicates the case is in a procedurally proper posture for the court to consider, a statement of the legal issues presented on appeal, a statement of the case that describes the procedural history of the case, a statement of facts that summarizes the legally significant facts at issue in the case, a summary of the argument that gives a concise explanation of the main points made in the argument, the argument itself, a separately headed conclusion, and a certificate of compliance that indicates that the brief complies with the court's printing and formatting requirements.[2]

Motions are another type of document that is often submitted to a court. A "motion" is a generic term used to describe any written document that asks a court to do something and is often the catchall term that lawyers use to title a document when there is no specific title for the document they are submitting to the court. Accordingly, motions can be very simple one-sentence requests or can be complex multipage requests with very involved legal analysis.

Sometimes, lawyers will draft a motion that requests the court to take a particular action, and then will attach a separate document titled a "Memorandum of Law" that details the legal analysis that supports the request made in the motion. Motions and memoranda of law are written in a persuasive manner because the lawyer is requesting a court to see the law and facts in the light that most favors the lawyer's client. Because motions are filed in existing cases, they must conform to the formatting requirements or customs of the courthouse that the motions are being submitted to.

Contracts, Leases, Wills, and Other Transactional Documents

There is a group of legal documents that are often referred to as "transactional documents" because instead of conducting a traditional legal analysis on a legal issue and then putting that analysis in written format for the benefit of a client, a court, or another lawyer, the lawyer is drafting a document that will actually be doing something for the client. Generally, the document establishes some sort of legal relationship with the third-party. These types of documents still require legal research because a lawyer has to discern what potential legal issues could arise if the document is drafted in particular ways.

---

2. Federal Rules of Appellate Procedure 28 & 32.

Also, these documents often have particular formatting requirements depending on the type of document that is being drafted, the legal requirements for recognition of that document in the jurisdiction where it will be used, and the customs that parties who frequently use these documents may have become used to. In addition to the traditional legal research that is conducted for any legal analysis, lawyers working on transactional documents often spend much time looking at similar previously drafted documents and consulting with lawyers that have worked on similar documents in order to ensure that the lawyer has thought through all the potential problems that could happen with the document once it is in use.

Law Reviews, Treatises, and Other Academic Documents

Lawyers are sometimes called on to write about the law from an academic perspective. Lawyers often write law review articles or books otherwise known as treatises. Sometimes lawyers will even write articles for magazines such as their local bar publications. Academic articles generally have a point or a thesis that the writer is trying to prove. In that sense, there is a bit of a persuasive element to academic writing. However, because of the academic nature of the writing, the persuasion is generally not nearly as heavy-handed as it would be if the document was being submitted to a court or opposing counsel. The particular customs and formatting for various academic publications are too individualized to discuss in any general nature, here. Lawyers typically look to examples of previously written documents in these publications in order to gauge the tone and substance of the document they are writing.

Determining the document that you are being asked to put together is the first step in a long list of decisions that you will need to make in order to write solid legal analysis that considers the science behind legal writing and the subjective artistry inherent in all writing. For instance, if the document is being submitted to a court, you should know that the tone of your explanation of the law will be more persuasive than if the document is being submitted to a judge you are clerking for.

It is important to understand the differences between the various types of legal writing because it may affect the applicability of the science discussed herein. For example, a lease document may not be improved by including emotional language. On the other hand, most court memoranda will benefit from considering the emotional impact of words used and the organizational structure of a sentence or paragraph.

Chapter 5

Deductive and Inductive Reasoning

Of all the topics in this book, perhaps the one that man has contemplated the longest is the art of argument. Philosophers in ancient times spent much time contemplating the "art" of persuasive language and how best to support arguments. But the "art" of argument, actually, has quite a lot of science behind it. Much of the argument that Socrates, Aristotle, and their contemporaries pontificated about while sitting on white marble steps of ancient Greek buildings is actually grounded in mathematical concepts.[1] This chapter will attempt to briefly explain those concepts.

There are two main types of guidance that courts give lawyers to understand how the court might rule on similar issues in the future—rules of law and factual decisions. The rules courts set out let attorneys know what courts will consider in future decisions. A lawyer can then apply those rules to a set of facts a client may bring to that lawyer. For example, a court may set forth the following rule: when a store knew or should have known that a dangerous condition that could harm customers was present in the store, the store has a duty to fix the condition immediately. That rule could help a lawyer know how to advise a client who is being sued by a customer who slipped and fell on a grape in the client's grocery store after the client was warned of the grape and failed to clean it up. However, if it isn't entirely clear how the rule applies in other situations, the lawyer may look for other guidance than just the rule. For instance, another client may come in to the lawyer's office and tell the lawyer she is being sued by a customer who slipped in her store on a grape that was on the floor for several hours, but the client was never actually told about the grape. The lawyer may struggle with answering the question of whether the client should have known about the grape because it was there for

---

1. Aristotle, PRIOR ANALYTICS, Book 1, Part 5, (1989).

several hours. Although there may be no rule from any case law guiding the lawyer to answer this question, if the court has decided a case that has similar facts to the client's facts, the lawyer may find some support in that case for how a court would decide whether the client should have known about the grape. Let's suppose the court decided that an auto parts store was at fault for a customer's fall when it failed to clean up a three-day-old spill of motor oil in an aisle because store personnel should have noticed the spill during that time. Based on the auto parts store case, the lawyer may be able to make an educated guess about what the court may do with the client's facts even if the court has not expressly created another rule. The lawyer may do this through indicating to the court that the client's facts are either similar or different to the facts of this case to support an interpretation of how the court will rule on the facts of the client's case.

Deductive (Syllogistic) Reasoning

The application of a rule to the facts at hand is an example of classic deductive reasoning, sometimes called syllogistic reasoning. This is the reasoning that Socrates spoke about and Aristotle and Plato later wrote about in their books on logic and rhetoric. These philosophers recognized the logical strength inherent in applying a rule, which these philosophers called a "Major Premise," to a set of facts that the rule affects, which these philosophers called a "Minor Premise." The classic example used by these philosophers is the following:

All men are mortal. (Major Premise)

Socrates is a man. (Minor Premise)

If these two statements are absolute truths, they force a reader to come to the inescapable conclusion that Socrates is mortal. The best rule applications follow a syllogistic structure. Here's an example of a rule application that follows a syllogistic structure:

A dog owner is liable for the injuries caused by the dog if a reasonable person would not have let the dog be unrestrained near people. (Major Premise)

A reasonable person would not have let Fido the dog off-leash near people. (Minor Premise)

Therefore, Fido's owner, Frank Smith, is liable for the injuries caused by Fido to Ms. Thomas. (Conclusion)

This argument structure not only has the support of philosophers, it also has mathematical support. The mathematical theory of transitivity supports the syllogistic structure as a sound logical tool. The theory of transitivity[2] is embodied by the following equation:

If A=B and B=C, then A=C

And the following Venn diagram:

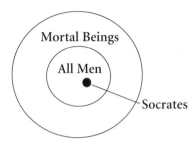

While mathematical concepts deal with absolutes like numbers, which always stand for the same thing, lawyers don't deal with absolutes. One jury's idea about what a "reasonable person" would do in a given situation may be different than another jury's idea about what a "reasonable person" would do. But aspiring to make an argument as close to an absolute equation is a goal every legal writer should strive for because the closer a legal writer can make an argument look to a mathematical concept, the less a court or an opposing counsel can quibble with the argument. Conversely, analyzing your argument and how closely it represents a mathematical concept can help a legal writer identify the inherent weaknesses of the argument.

When a legal writer does identify an area where the written word is far afield from a mathematical absolute, the legal writer can attempt to "ground" that premise to make it more logically sound. For instance, if there is case law that indicates a reasonable person would never let a dog off-leash when the dog had bitten someone before, the following syllogism could ground the Minor Premise of the Fido syllogism:

A reasonable person would not let a dog off-leash around people if that dog has a history of biting people. (Major Premise)

Fido had a history of biting people. (Minor Premise)

A reasonable person would not have let Fido off-leash. (Conclusion)

2. Gray Pilgrim, *Transitive Property*, http://www.buzzle.com/articles/transitive-property.html (last visited 2/28/2014).

There are many reasons why a legal writer's argument may be far more verbose than the syllogisms that underlie the argument, but making the effort to reduce the prose of an argument to a simple syllogistic form can help a writer analyze the premises that need to be grounded as well as assisting with organizational considerations. If a syllogism is grounded by another syllogism, the latter syllogism needs to be explained before the former. Grounding the "reasonable person" standard in the "Fido" syllogism will prevent the reader from questioning the "reasonable person" standard when presented in the "Fido" syllogism.

Because language is not an "absolute" like a mathematical principle, an attorney can craft a perfectly logical syllogism based on illogical statements that undermine the logical affect of the syllogism. For example,

All dogs are cats.

Fido is a dog.

Therefore, Fido is a cat.

As you can see, following a syllogistic structure only ensures that your argument is logically sound if the premises you used in the syllogism are true and logical.

Inductive Reasoning

Although rule applications are the preferred method of logical argument because of their long rhetorical history and their internal logical soundness, rules can only take analysis so far in some situations. For instance, sometimes courts do not fully explain their reasoning as a "rule," but instead simply find that certain facts rise to the level of an expressed rule. Suppose the court that wrote the opinion you were using to analyze the Fido facts was clear that the rule it was applying was the following:

A dog owner is liable for the injuries caused by their dog if a reasonable person would not have let the dog be unrestrained near people.

The court then found that a reasonable person would not allow a dog off-leash who had bitten someone before, but stopped short of indicating that was a rule to be applied in every case going forward. So instead of presenting it as a syllogistic rule that applies in every situation, you feel better about simply listing the "reasonable person" rule and then indicating that our facts are similar to the precedent case facts. You plan to go further and indicate that our court should then find, like the precedent court, that a reasonable person would not have let the dog off-leash. This type of analysis is a classic factual comparison. It is also an example of inductive reasoning. Inductive reasoning attempts to predict the outcome of a new problem by looking at the outcome and assuming that outcome will happen again. A classic example of inductive reasoning is the following:

> My grapefruit have ripened in January every year for the last ten years.

> Therefore, my grapefruit will ripen in January this year.

The inherent problem with inductive reasoning is that there are lots of reasons why events happen in a certain manner and a change in those reasons may make the outcome different in a new situation. For instance, this may be the year that there is a particularly cold winter, so the grapefruit do not ripen in January. Therefore even if it is true that the grapefruit have ripened in January, it doesn't mean that there is an inescapable conclusion that the grapefruit will ripen this year in January. In the legal realm, fact comparisons are usually made by attorneys when the court isn't clear in an opinion about its reasons for deciding that a certain set of facts meets a legal rule. So any guess at why the court made that decision is simply that: a guess. And there is a chance that the court made that decision for a reason that isn't applicable to a new set of facts.

To return to our "Fido" example, the court may have found that it wasn't reasonable to let the dog off-leash in the precedent case because the dog was a large dog and previously bit somebody, but didn't expressly state those as the reasons in the opinion. If Fido is a Chihuahua, then this same court may have found it was reasonable to let Fido off-leash even if he had bitten someone before because Fido is a small dog. Because of the inherent weakness of inductive reasoning, this argument structure may not be as preferred as deductive (or "syllogistic" reasoning). But, if the authoritative case law you have to work with does not contain the rules, rationale, and reasoning behind the Court's decision, inductive reasoning may be the strongest argument structure you can use and is a wise choice in that instance.

Sidebar: Rule Application versus Factual Comparisons

As noted in the introduction to this section, lawyers use two main modes of application of cases to new facts. A court may express a general rule that is applicable in similar situations and an attorney can apply that rule to a new set of facts. Sometimes, the court does not clearly express a rule, but an attorney extrapolates a rule from the way the court rules on the facts of the case. The slip and fall inside of a store explained in the introduction is a good example of this. An attorney could argue that the case involving the spilled oil on the auto parts store stands for the rule that if a long enough time elapsed with the spill on the store floor, the store should have known about the spill and is therefore liable for a slip and fall. In the alternative, the attorney could build an argument on factual comparisons between the client's facts and the facts of the auto parts case. For example, the attorney could say that unlike the auto parts case, the grape in the client's case was only on the floor a few hours. Accordingly, the attorney can argue a court should find that the client is not liable for the slip and fall, despite what the court found in the auto parts case. Whether you use a syllogism to build an argument based on applying a rule or inductive reasoning to build an argument based on factual comparisons will largely be a function of preference, but here are some considerations that may help you decide which method to use.

• Can you fairly extrapolate a rule? Only if you are confident that the court used a rule in deciding a case as it did, can you use that rule to form the basis of a syllogism.

• Is there enough space to use arguments based on both a syllogism and a fact comparison? If it is a strong point of your analysis, you may want to do both.

• Generally, syllogisms are more logically sound because of the mathematical propositions of syllogisms explained in the section of this chapter on that topic. However, if the facts are particularly similar or strikingly opposite, you may find that a factual comparison is more powerful.

Whichever method you choose to describe your analysis, make sure you have described it in the best way possible by analyzing the logical steps a reader would need to process your syllogism or indicative reasoning and have explained those steps well.

Deductive and Inductive Reasoning Exercise

Take a look at the following example of a portion of an internal office memo regarding appropriate jurisdiction in a contract dispute between Hanson Hardware Store and one of its suppliers, Barcom Plumbing Supply, LLC.

> A company has fair warning that it is subject to the jurisdiction of a state court when the company establishes minimum contacts in the state. Barcom Plumbing Supply, LLC conducted prior negotiations and contemplated future consequences in Illinois. Additionally, Barcom established minimum contacts with an Illinois company because its conduct and connection with the forum state were such that the company should have reasonably anticipated being haled into court there. Barcom acted much like the company in the aforementioned *Smith* case when it contracted to Hanson to sell plumbing fixtures in any of its stores, many of which are in the state of Illinois. Therefore, Barcom has established minimum contacts with Illinois and as a result, Barcom has fair warning that it is subject to Illinois state court jurisdiction.

Can you identify the type of logical structure employed by this writer? Is the writer employing syllogistic reasoning? If so, is the syllogistic structure logically correct? Does the writer employ inductive reasoning? If so, is it clear what the premises are that form the basis of the inductive reasoning? Do you think the writer could explain these arguments in a more logically sound manner? Can you write this paragraph in a manner that better explains the reasoning that seems to be behind this argument? Based on your observations, what do you think a writer needs to do to clearly explain syllogistic and inductive reasoning?

Chapter 6

Which Type of Legal Reasoning Works Best?

As discussed in Chapter 5, deductive reasoning and syllogistic logic, together with inductive reasoning and the use of analogy, form the traditional backbone of legal writing and analysis. The interplay between deductive and inductive reasoning drives the majority of legal writing.[1] Recently, however, focus has been given to other types of legal reasoning; legal scholars have noted that much legal reasoning is based on logical fallacies (ad hominem arguments for example) and other forms of legal reasoning that are not a part of the deductive or inductive model.

Legal writing textbooks reflect the emphasis on traditional forms of legal writing. Most espouse the same concepts for effective legal reasoning: rule-based reasoning (deductive reasoning) and analogical reasoning (inductive reasoning), but add other types of reasoning as well, such as policy-based reasoning, and even narrative reasoning. Nevertheless, the most advocated of these concepts are rule-based and analogical reasoning. Rule-based reasoning relies on the language of a rule or group of rules to predict an outcome whereas analogical relies on a comparison to prior case law to make a prediction.

It is believed that legal analysis relies heavily on rule-based reasoning because rule-based reasoning clarifies the precise language, structure, and meaning of a rule.[2] Of all forms of reasoning available in legal writing, rule-based reasoning is the most common form because it requires applying predetermined rules to a specific set of facts.[3] Rule-based reasoning is used when a rule is so clear that its application raises no questions and when no analogous case

---

1. David S. Romantz & Kathleen Elliott Vinson, *Legal Analysis: The Fundamental Skill* 1, Pinpoint (2d ed., 2009).
2. Linda H. Edwards, *Legal Writing and Analysis* 119 (2d ed., 2007).
3. Michael D. Murray & Christy H. DeSanctis, *Legal Writing and Analysis* at 19 (2d ed., 2009).

exists.[4] Therefore, it can be effective if done correctly and is arguably the best place to start when forming a legal argument.[5]

Analogical reasoning, which is also sometimes called "inductive" reasoning, is often used as an attempt to link the case at hand to other similar cases in which the outcome was favorable, or when necessary, to distinguish the case where the outcome was unfavorable.[6] It is believed that, whether a case is analogized or distinguished, the process should happen in three steps: making sure the precedent is the same as the issue at hand, looking at the determinative facts, and comparing those determinative facts to the facts of the current case.[7] As far as the effectiveness of analogical reasoning, only probable proof for the conclusions reached can be offered, not certainty.[8] However, analogical reasoning is believed to be compelling because it is powered by stare decisis and because stare decisis requires a court to reach a particular outcome. There is also the idea of using rule-based and analogical reasoning together; combining the two approaches strengthens the argument, especially where a direct application of the rule alone would not be clear, or if there is no applicable case law.[9]

Policy-based legal reasoning is another popular method of legal reasoning. The central question when forming a policy-based argument is "what could a court do that would satisfy not just the elements of a rule, but also the reason why the rule exists in the first place—its policy?"[10] Policy can be found expressly stated in statutes but it is usually found in case law. It is believed policy-based reasoning is most often used to reinforce an argument that is supported by primary authorities.[11] This form of reasoning involves arguing that X is the answer but not just because the authorities had X result but because X satisfies the policies important to the particular area of law.[12]

Similar to policy-based reasoning, principle-based reasoning is another common form of legal reasoning. Principle-based legal reasoning attempts to

---

4. Christine Coughlin et al., A Lawyer Writes: A Practical Guide to Legal Analysis 132 (2008).

5. Edwards, *supra* n. 2, at 43.

6. Murray & DeSanctis, *supra* n. 3, at 21.

7. Richard K. Neumann, Jr. & Sheila Simon, Legal Writing 54 (2d ed., 2011).

8. Helene S. Shapo et al., Writing and Analysis in the Law 63 (5th ed., 2008).

9. Coughlin, et al., *supra* n. 4 at.

10. Richard K. Neumann, Jr. supra n.7, at 56.

11. Murray & DeSanctis, *supra* n. 3, at 22

12. *Id.* at 22–23.

identify any principles that a rule is trying to serve or that might constrain the interpretation of a rule.[13] This type of legal reasoning is best used when trying to explain a rule's purpose.[14] When using principle-based reasoning, the argument focuses on X as the answer because X upholds the principles (morality, justice, freedom, etc.) that the rule was meant to protect.[15]

Recently, much scholarly legal writing has been directed towards narrative as an effective form of legal writing, and according to some scholars and researchers, the most persuasive form of legal analysis.[16] Narrative as a form of legal persuasion is discussed in Chapter 10.

To a certain extent, the type of law used dictates the type of reasoning employed.[17] For example, the primary reasoning tactic used in common law analysis is analogical reasoning.[18] However, when analyzing a statute, the text of the statutory rule tends to be more important than principles of stare decisis.[19]

One helpful categorization of legal reasoning methodologies has been put forth by Wilson Huhn in his article, *Teaching Legal Analysis Using a Pluralistic Model of Law*. Huhn suggests the five types of legal arguments are: text, intent, precedent, tradition, and policy analysis.[20] Text dates back to when written words recorded the rights and obligations of parties to a feudal contract, and as a legal argument, text meant that when something was written it would be considered binding law.[21] Text analysis requires interpreting the language by its plain meaning, intratextual arguments, or other canons of construction.[22] Regardless of which method of interpretation is used, the goal is to achieve an objective definition of the words of the text.[23] The second type of legal argument focuses on the intent of those who wrote the text. This could be the in-

---

13. Edwards, *supra* n. 2 at 119.

14. *Id.*

15. *Id.* at 59

16. Kenneth D. Chestek, *Judging By the Numbers: An Empirical Study of the Power of Story*, 7 J. ALWD 1, 2 (2010).

17. John C. Dernbach et. al., *A Practical Guide to Legal Writing & Legal Method*, 111 (4th ed., Aspen 2010).

18. *Id.* at 96.

19. *Id.* at 111.

20. Wilson R. Huhn, *Teaching Legal Analysis Using a Pluralistic Model of Law*, 36:3 GONZ. L. REV. 433, 440 (2000–2001).

21. *Id.* at 440–41.

22. *Id.* at 441–42.

23. *Id.* at 442–43.

tent of the Framers when looking at constitutional law, or regulatory intent when looking at agency rules, or even intent of the parties to a contract.[24]

The third source of law is precedent. "The principle of stare decisis is what lends strength to precedent." After declaring "[l]iberty finds no refuge in a jurisprudence of doubt," Justices O'Connor, Kennedy, and Souter articulated guidelines for determining when constitutional precedent must be allowed and when it may be overruled.[25] A fourth source of legal authority is tradition. "The Supreme Court has identified 'tradition' as the touchstone for determining our fundamental rights."[26]

Finally, there is policy analysis. Policy analysis requires two steps: a predictive statement and an evaluative judgment.[27] This type of analysis asks the court to predict the consequences that will arise from interpreting the law one way versus the other, and then determining which resulting consequence would be more consistent with the underlying values of the law.[28]

After reading the foregoing explanation of the various types of legal reasoning, you are undoubtedly excited to learn which of the several types of legal reasoning is the best. (Spoiler alert: If you don't want to know the answer, do not read the next sentence until you read the rest of the chapter.) The answer is, there is no answer. While professors, scientists, and scholars have all suggested that one of the several types of legal reasoning may be superior, to our knowledge, nobody has yet done a study suggesting that one is better than the others. Most legal writing scholars acknowledge that there is little scientific and empirical data on legal writing per se, and much of the scientific analysis of legal writing relies on psychological, behavioral, and social science research.[29] Recently, such scholarship has made significant progress in applying science and empirical analysis to legal writing,[30] and legal writing conferences have

----

24. *Id.* at 443.

25. *Id.* at 444–45.

26. *Id.* at 445.

27. *Id.* at 449.

28. *Id.* at 449.

29. *See e.g.* Melissa H. Weresh, *Morality, Trust, and Illusion: Ethos as Relationship*, 9 Legal Commun. & Rhetoric: JALWD 229 (2012) (utilizing and applying social psychology studies to show the role of ethos (credibility established through a relationship of trust) in legal writing); and Kathryn Stanchi, *Playing with Fire: The Science of Confronting Adverse Material in Legal Advocacy*, 60 Rutgers L. Rev. 381(2008), *The Power of Priming in Legal Advocacy: Using the Science of First Impressions to Persuade the Reader*, 89 Or. L. Rev. 305 (2010), *Teaching Students to Present Law Persuasively Using Techniques from Psychology*, 19 Persp.: Teaching Legal Res. & Writing 142 (2011).

30. *Id.*

emphasized the role science and empirical data play in helping us understand and improve legal writing.[31]

The good news is that the research that does support various types of legal arguments, including some of the research cited in this chapter, is discussed throughout the rest of the book.

---

31. One such conference was "A Dialogue About Persuasion in Legal Writing & Lawyering" held on September 19, 2008 at Rutgers School of Law—Camden. A summary of the conference can be found at Legal Writing Prof Blog: http://lawprofessors.typepad.com/legal-writing/2008/09/page/2/. Another was a symposium entitled "The Impact of Cognitive Bias on Persuasion and Writing Strategies" held on March 1, 2013 at Brooklyn Law School. The papers from the symposium can be found at 22 J.L. & Pol'y 1 (2013).

PART III
Concepts for Writing All Legal Documents

Chapter 7

Does Format Matter?

At this point in the book, it may seem like using the science behind the art of legal writing to improve the persuasiveness of your writing might require a fair amount of work. And this is usually true—except for the science in this chapter. Finally, here is something that science shows will improve the persuasiveness of your writing without scarcely any effort on your part.

Studies show that a writer can increase the persuasiveness of a legal document simply by making a few format changes. While a writer of legal documents might not always have control over the format of the documents written, to the extent it is in the writer's control, it is also in the writer's best interest to know what aspects of design and format make a difference persuasively and to use that information advantageously.[1]

While often taken for granted, fonts play an important role in the conveyance of words. An entire discipline—typography—exists to study the best ways to lay out a typeface. Which font to use is a subject of much debate—and often personal preference—so it is best for a writer to know the audience when selecting a font. Research has shown that some fonts are more believable than others,[2] and there are other components of fonts and formatting to take into consideration when creating a document.

First, many courts, offices, and other institutions have rules or guidelines on what font, paper size, margin size, or spacing a document must use.[3] Before becoming too creative, it is important to make sure you follow those rules so as not to have your submission discarded, rejected, or overlooked (or overly

---

1. Chris Gayomali, *How Typeface Influences the Way We Read and Think: And Why Everyone Hates Comic Sans MS*, The Week (June 14, 2013), http://theweek.com/article/index/245632/how-typeface-influences-the-way-we-read-and-think.

2. Suzanne Labarre, Fast Co. Design, *Are Some Fonts More Believable Than Others?* (Aug 16, 2012), http://www.fastcodesign.com/1670556/are-some-fonts-more-believable-than-others.

3. Matthew Butterick, Typography for Lawyers (2010). Parts of this book are also available at http://typographyforlawyers.com/index.html.

scrutinized); failure to follow these guidelines would negate any hoped for persuasive benefit.

But, when there isn't much control over how a document can look, there are subtle things a writer can do to make the submission more appealing. First, will the reader likely be reading it on a screen (computer, tablet, phone) or on a print copy? While subject to some debate, it is generally believed that sans serif fonts (those without the little flourishes at the ends of the letters, like arial) are more suitable for reading on a screen, while serif fonts (those with the little flourishes, like the font you are reading) are better suited for print.[4] Second, think about how important it is for your document to be read in the exact format in which you send it. For example, it is normally preferable to send an electronic copy of a document in PDF form, as it is most likely to retain the visual quality as you saw it on your screen when viewed on someone else's screen.

Even though there are many factors a writer can consider when trying to choose persuasive formatting, such as spacing between letters, lengths of lines, spacing between lines, contrast with backgrounds, the "x-height" of a font, the choice of fonts when using multiple fonts (limit yourself to two or three different fonts),[5] or using headers, graphics, or any other visual material, the easiest thing a writer can do to guarantee a more persuasive document is to choose the right font.

Apparently, using the wrong font, such as Comic Sans MS, for announcing groundbreaking scientific research can have serious repercussions:

> The hunt for the Higgs boson [the "God" particle] was one of the most expensive and labor-intensive particle physics projects ever undertaken, and promised to answer the fundamental but elusive question of why our atoms stick together in the first place. And yet, when CERN researchers finally announced that they'd glimpsed the Higgs, the world's first reaction wasn't to cheer; it was to stifle collective laughter. The institution's scientists, cradling the most important scientific discovery of the decade, had chosen to present their findings to a breathless public using a peculiar font face: Comic Sans MS.[6]

---

4. Alex Poole, *Which Are More Legible: Serif or Sans Serif Typefaces?* (Aug. 17, 2008), http://alexpoole.info/blog/which-are-more-legible-serif-or-sans-serif-typefaces/.

5. See Susan Hilligoss and Theron Howard, *Visual Communication, A Writer's Guide,* 121–32 (2002).

6. Chris Gayomali, *How Typeface Influences the Way We Read and Think,* THE WEEK, http://theweek.com/article/index/245632/how-typeface-influences-the-way-we-read-and-think.

In case you are wondering, Comic Sans MS looks like this. Apparently, Fabiola Gianotti, the CERN coordinator, just liked the font,[7] and was unaware of the now statistically-proven fact that Comic Sans MS is one of the least credible (but one of the cutest) fonts.

So, now you know which font not to use for your brief. But, if you knew you could have a statistically significant guarantee that your writing would be more credible by using a certain font, would you use it? The good news is that there is such a guarantee, and using this guaranteed font will provide a huge, well, maybe not huge, but a substantial, no, not that either, but at least *a slight* edge on the believability and credibility of your written work product. All you need to do is use the font named "Baskerville."

Yes, it's that simple, according to research performed by *New York Times* writer Errol Morris and Cornell Psychologist David Dunning. "Baskerville's weighted advantage wasn't huge—just 1.5 percent. That advantage may seem small," Dunning told the Times, "but if that was a bump up in sales figures, many online companies would kill for it. The fact that font matters at all is a wonderment."[8]

The research involved responses from 40,000 people responding to an online quiz about a science article. The quiz asked whether the respondent thought the article was believable. The science article, of course, was written in different typefaces, including Comic Sans MS and Baskerville. And, as you guessed, the respondents that received the article written in Baskerville, found it more believable.[9] While the difference is not huge, it takes very little effort to change a font. See, we just did it; we changed to Baskerville and it was easy, and now this sentence is much more—1.5% more, to be exact— believable.

Other appropriate fonts for particular legal documents, as well as fonts that should never be used **(Comic Sans MS is one of them)**, can be found in the bible of legal typography: *Typography for Lawyers* by Matthew Butterick. Butterick also tells you why the ubiquitous Times New Roman was not meant for legal writing[10] and how many different fonts you should use in a single document.[11]

---

7. Errol Morris, *Hear, All Ye People; Hearken, O Earth (Part One)*, N.Y. TIMES http://opinionator.blogs.nytimes.com/2012/08/08/hear-all-ye-people-hearken-o-earth/?_r=0.

8. *Id.*

9. *Id.*

10. *Id.*

11. *Id.*

Now, there is one little catch. While all of the above-cited research seems focused on helping you format your document, and in particular, pick a font that is more "readable," there is a little piece of research that suggests that if you want to help your reader better comprehend your document—not just read it—but comprehend it, you should use a typeface that is harder to read.

This somewhat counter-intuitive statement is supported by a 2007 study by several psychologists who gave two versions of a test called the Cognitive Reflection Test (CRT) to Princeton students.[12] The CRT, developed by Princeton Professor Shane Frederick, measures a specific cognitive ability to suppress a spontaneous and intuitive response (and wrong answer) in favor of a more deliberative and reflective correct answer. The test has only three questions for which the spontaneous response is incorrect, but the respondents can generally answer all three questions correctly by taking more time to deliberate. A correct response on a question suggests that the respondent used systemic processing to correct their spontaneous or intuitive response.

For example: A bat and a ball cost $1.10 total. The bat costs $1.00 more than the ball. How much does the ball cost? _____ cents. The quick answer most people give is "10 cents", which is incorrect. Those who were more deliberate in their answering figured out the correct answer, which is "5 cents."[13]

Professor Frederick gave the CRT to 3,400 participants in 35 studies. He demonstrated that scores on the CRT were highly correlated with intelligence and analytical thinking skills. Professors Alter, Oppenheimer, Epley, and Eyre then took Frederick's study and manipulated it to show that people "adopt a systemic approach to reasoning when they experience cognitive disfluency."[14] Using Frederick's same CRT test questions, the conditions of the test were changed through the use of a different font for half of the participants. A standard, easy-to-read black Myriad Web 12-point font (which was "fluent") was changed to a difficult-to-read 10 percent gray italicized Myriad Web 10-point font (which was disfluent).

For example: A bat and a ball cost $1.10 total. The bat costs $1.00 more than the ball. How much does the ball cost? _____ cents. (Fluent.) *On the other hand: A bat and a ball cost $1.10 total. The bat costs $1.00 more than the ball. How much does the ball cost? _____ cents. (Disfluent.)*

---

12. Adam L. Alter and Daniel M. Oppenheimer Nicholas Epley Rebecca N. Eyre, *Overcoming Intuition: Metacognitive Difficulty Activates Analytic Reasoning* Journal of Experimental Psychology: 2007, Vol. 136, No. 4, 569–576.

13. Shane Frederick, *Cognitive Reflection and Decision Making.* Journal of Economic Perspectives, 19(4): 25–42 (2005).

14. Alter, *supra* n. 13, at 570.

Alter, Oppenheimer, Epley, and Eyre predicted that under disfluent conditions, more of the CRT questions would be answered correctly,[15] and they were right. Participants answered more items correctly on the CRT with the disfluent font than with the fluent font. The study found 90 percent of participants with the fluent font answered at least one question wrong but only 35 percent did so with the disfluent conditions. The results provided preliminary evidence that disfluency (which can be caused by numerous factors, not just font changes) initiates systemic or higher reasoning processes.[16]

So, if you want a reader to read your written text carefully, then choose a font that is hard to read. If, on the other hand you want the reader to be able to quickly understand your writing—even at the cost of not completely comprehending it to the depth that might be engendered by a hard-to-read text, then stick with a credible, easy-to-read font. Our advice is to go for an easy-to-read font that will enable the reader to quickly read a document. By using a hard-to-read font, you risk angering a reader and losing your credibility. Your credibility as a writer is probably more important for your own welfare and for the welfare of your client than better initial comprehension. So, format does matter, and the easiest way to produce a credible format is to use a credible, easy-to-read font.

---

15. *Id.*
16. *Id.* at 570–71.

Chapter 8

Does Correct Grammar Matter?

Twenty years ago, the question posed by the chapter title would have been considered almost absurd. It could only have been answered with a resounding "Yes, of course—what kind of a question is that?" Today, the question is no longer absurd, and the answer is no longer as clear as it would have been in the twentieth century. Today's law students find themselves in an interesting situation. Their writing has, for the most part, been less formal than the writing of previous generations of law students. Texting, emails, tweets, instagrams, and other less formal forms of writing constitute a large portion of current law students' writing experience. Unfortunately, as future lawyers, they will still be writing to judges, senior partners, and clients who grew up in a pre-electronic era and who are much more likely to be concerned about correct grammar.

For example, one survey showed that 70% of Australian employers were dissatisfied with Generation Y's grammar usage.[1] And (note that I started a sentence with "and," a non-traditional usage for beginning a sentence), although many of today's grammarians and legal writing experts are not as concerned about correct traditional grammar as previous generations of grammarians,[2] others are. So, how much concern should today's law student have for learning and applying traditional "correct" rules of grammar?

The answer remains unchanged, although the strength of the answer has changed: Grammar usage errors *do* have an effect on a reader's opinion of a writer,

---

1. Smart Company, *Who'd Hire a Gen-Y* http://www.smartcompany.com.au/people/recruitment/7341-who-d-hire-a-gen-y.html (July 12, 2007).

2. NY Times, *Which Language Rules to Flout or Flaunt* http://www.nytimes.com/roomfordebate/2012/09/27/which-language-and-grammar-rules-to-flout (Sep. 27, 2012); Chronicle of Higher Educ. *Fifty Years of Stupid Grammar Advice*, http://chronicle.com/article/50-Years-of-Stupid-Grammar/25497 (April 17, 2009).

but not as much as they did thirty-some years ago. Reactions vary depending on severity and range from "status marking" loss of respect to mild annoyance. Women tend to be more critical than men, and older respondents more critical than younger respondents. The "status marking," or most outrageous errors, have remained constant through the years though "botheration" in general has steadily declined.[3]

Thirty-two years ago, in 1981, Maxine Hairston performed a landmark study of the responses of "nonacademic readers in the professions" to various grammatical errors read by the study's respondents.[4] Hairston ranked the perceived seriousness of various grammatical errors as "status markers," "very serious," "fairly serious," "medium to low," and "bother[ed] only a very few people."[5] Outrageous ("status marking") errors are those involving a nonstandard past or past-participle verb form (brung, has went), a lack of subject-verb agreement in certain cases (we was), double negatives (never been nobody), and an object pronoun as subject (Him and Richard).[6]

Very serious errors include sentence fragments, fused (run-on) sentences (he concentrated on his job he never took vacations), noncapitalization of proper nouns, misspellings (including contractions like "would of"), lack of subject-verb agreement in other cases (enclosed in his personnel file is his papers), a comma between the verb and its complement (Cox cannot predict, that street crime will diminish), nonparallelism, (impressed by her smooth manner elegant clothes, and being witty), faulty adverb form (treated his men bad), and misuse of transitive verbs (if the agency sets down on the job).[7]

Serious errors include faulty predication (the policy intimidates hiring), dangling modifiers (having argued all morning, a decision was finally reached), subject pronoun used as an object pronoun (the army moved my husband and I), lack of commas to set off interrupters (when the time came to pay the fee however the candidate withdrew), lack of commas in a series, tense switching (the reporter paid attention to officers but ignores enlisted men), use of a plural determiner with a singular noun (these kind of errors), and lack of pronoun-antecedent agreement (everyone who attends will have to pay their own expenses).[8] The following list summarizes Hairston's findings:

---

3. *Id.*

4. Maxine Hairston, *Not All Errors Are Created Equal: Nonacademic Readers in the Professions Respond to Lapses in Usage*, 43 C. Eng. 794, 795 (1981).

5. *Id.* at 796–97.

6. Hairston, *supra* n.6, at 796–98.

7. *Id.* at 797. The examples are taken from the Hairston study.

8. *Id.*

Decrease of 20% or more:

- Noncapitalization
- Subject pronoun used as object
- Lack of pronoun-antecedent agreement
- Dangling modifiers
- Object pronoun as predicate nominative
- Lack of possessive determiner before a gerund
- Use of a plural modifier with a singular noun

Decrease of 10% or more:

- Nonstandard past-participle verb form
- Double negatives
- Object pronoun as subject
- Misspelling
- Misplaced comma (verb and complement)
- Faulty predication
- Lack of comma to set off an absolute
- Nonparallelism
- Sentence fragments
- Lack of subjunctive mood
- Colon after linking verb
- Collocation mistake
- Qualifier before a non-gradable adjective

Less serious errors included "not using the possessive form before a gerund, failure to set off an appositive with commas, not using quotation marks appropriately, using 'If I was' instead of 'If I were'... failure to set off introductory clauses with commas, using 'whoever' in a sentence that called for 'whomever'... and not distinguishing between *among* and *between*." Comma splices were also less serious.[9] The least bothersome errors included "writing 'different than' instead of 'different from,' using a singular verb with 'data, ... and omitting the apostrophe in the contraction 'it's.'"[10]

Twenty-two years later, Loretta Gray and Paula Heuser replicated Hairston's study and found that the same nonacademic readers found the same types of errors less bothersome.[11] But, unlike Hairston's study, this time women were not more critical than men. Interestingly, the status marking or very serious errors were the same, but most categories were less bothersome overall.[12]

---

9. *Id.*

10. *Id.*

11. Loretta S. Gray & Paula Heuser, *Nonacademic Professionals' Perception of Usage Errors*, 22 J. of Basic Writing 50 (2003).

12. *Id.* at 57–58.

A similar conclusion was reached by another study published in 2001 by Jeanette Gilsdorf and Don Leonard, which compared a 1990 study with a 2001 study and found that business executives were less bothered by questionable usage elements and that younger readers were less bothered than older readers.[13] While the usage elements considered by Gilsdorf and Leonard did not necessarily correspond with those used by Hairston and Gray and Heuser, and the Gilsdorf and Leonard study did not even consider the most serious errors addressed by Hairston, the study found that women were more critical than men; however, that could be because more of the women surveyed were academics.[14] The authors summarized their advice to students:

> If your organization doesn't want you to start a sentence with "but" or end a sentence with a preposition, then avoid doing so. The rule that prevails is adaptation to one's audience. When there are other correct options, one need not use a displeasing language form merely because it happens also to be correct.[15]

In other words, write to your audience. Generally, readers are less concerned with grammar and usage errors today than thirty years ago. In Hairston's study 79/80 respondents said that egregious errors bothered them a lot. They were "outrageous"![16] In Gray and Heuser's study these errors still bothered almost all respondents, but about 20% less thought they were only "very serious."[17] Gilsdorf and Leonard found that professionals and academics alike are most bothered by sentence structure errors.[18] These errors were predominant in Hairston's "very serious" category and decreased in botheration by only 10% according to Gray and Heuser.[19]

The bottom line for today's legal writer is that ample evidence exists to show that even though there is less concern about technical grammar usage today when compared with the concern that existed thirty or even ten years ago, there is still enough concern about grammar to err on the side of knowing and using conventional grammar.

---

13. Jeannette Gilsdorf & Don Leonard, *Big Stuff, Little Stuff: A Decennial Measurement of Executives' and Academics' Reactions to Questionable Usage Elements*, 38 J. OF BUS. COMM. 439 (October 2001).

14. *Id.*

15. *Id.*

16. Hairston, *supra* n.6, at 796.

17. Gray & Heuser, *supra* n. 13 at 58.

18. Gilsdorf & Leonard , *supra* n. 15.

19. Gray & Heuser, *supra* n. 13 at 55.

Chapter 9

Readability and Plain Language[*]

Does the readability of your legal writing affect its effectiveness in legal memoranda submitted to a court? The short answer is "no"—at least if by "readability" you mean readability as judged by two of the several well-recognized readability formulas developed by researchers during the past fifty or sixty years. Using the Flesch Reading Ease scale and the Flesch-Kincaid Grade-Level scale, a recent study by Professors Long and Christensen analyzed the readability of 882 state, federal, and United States Supreme Court briefs and found no statistically significant relationship between the readability of those briefs and success on appeal.[1]

This is good news for those who would like to believe that appeals are decided on the merits of a case and that the success of an appeal is not influenced by the "readability" of a brief (or by any other writing convention, for that matter). It is also good news for critics of readability formulas, who may believe either that such formulas are fundamentally flawed or that such formulas have little to do with legal writing. It provides readability critics with yet another argument for disregarding readability analyses (even if readability is valid, it doesn't make a quantifiable difference). On the other hand, this may be less welcome news for legal writing professionals who may want to believe that the likelihood of success on appeal can be increased by writing a more "readable" brief and that a computerized readability formula can provide a basis for determining readability.[2]

---

[*] This chapter is adapted from Lance N. Long and William F. Christensen, *Does the Readability of Your Brief Affect Your Chance of Winning an Appeal?* 12 Journal of Appellate Practice & Process 145 (Spring 2011).

1. *Id.*

2. Of course, not all legal writing professionals share this belief. In particular, Professor Sirico has noted that unless readability formulas are properly understood and implemented, reliance on them can be counterproductive. *See generally* Louis J. Sirico, Jr., *Readability Studies: How Technocentrism Can Compromise Research and Legal Determinations*, 26 Quinnipiac L. Rev. 147 (2007). Our findings, although based on a formula that he criticizes, suggest that Flesch readability has little applicability to appellate brief success.

Most legal writing texts urge students to use short, concise sentences and to avoid a longer word when a shorter one will work.[3] For example, a legal writer should use "after" rather than "subsequent to" and "when" rather than "at such a time as."

The Long/Christensen study was an attempt to determine whether using long sentences and long words correlated with success on appeal. The Flesch readability formulas used in the study measure precisely those two elements. The study was not particularly concerned about whether readability formulas accurately measured the appropriateness of a particular text for a particular reader. Appellate briefs, no matter how readable or unreadable they may be, are read by a highly educated audience. But for all readers, including highly educated readers, it is generally easier to read shorter sentences and shorter words.[4] Could this possibly make a difference in the outcome of an appeal?

The Long/Christensen study suggested that the length of sentences and words, which is "readability" for the study's purposes, probably does not make much difference in appellate brief writing. First, they found that most briefs are written at about the same level of readability; there simply is not much difference in how lawyers write appellate briefs when it comes to the length of sentences and words. Furthermore, the readability of most appellate briefs is well within the reading ability of the highly educated audience of appellate judges and justices. Second, the relatively small differences in readability were not related to the outcome of an appeal in a statistically significant manner. The study did show, however, that the opinions of judges and justices were less readable than lawyers' briefs and that the opinions of dissenting judges or justices are the least readable of all the appellate writing analyzed. Ultimately, the study concluded that readability, as determined by the Flesch Reading Ease scale, was a non-issue for legal writing at the appellate level. Although read-

---

3. See e.g. Linda H. Edwards, *Legal Writing and Analysis* 281–85 (Wolters Kluwer 2011); Nancy L. Schultz & Louis J. Sirico, Jr., *Legal Writing and Other Lawyering Skills* 98–99 (Aspen 2010); Michael D. Murray & Christy H. DeSanctis, *Legal Writing and Analysis* 242 (Foundation Press 2009). Noah A. Messing offers a particularly detailed analysis of using short words and sentences, including an exhaustive list of monosyllabic verbs in *The Art of Advocacy* 247–48 and Appendix C (Wolters Kluwer 2013).

4. See generally Peter M. Tiersma, *Legal Language* 219–20 (U. of Chicago Press 1999) (noting that even appellate judges may be befuddled by the language of the typical insurance contract); Rudolf Flesch, *How to Write Plain English, A Book for Lawyers and Consumers* 20–22 (Harper & Row 1979) (discussing this phenomenon and concluding by noting that "the longer a sentence, the harder it is to read"); see also n. 38, infra.

ability did not appear to be related to outcome, there was a statistically significant relationship between the readability of the courts' majority and dissenting opinions.[5] Dissenting opinions were decidedly less readable than majority opinions.[6]

It is beyond the scope of this chapter to fully examine and explain readability formulas or the history and theory behind those formulas.[7] A short summary of the concept of readability, however, is provided here to explain the purpose of readability formulas.

" 'Readability' is what makes some texts easier to read than others."[8] Since the 1920s, researchers, including linguists, educators, psychologists, and other scholars, have analyzed writing to determine what makes it more or less readable.[9] By the 1950s, several formulas for assessing readability had been developed, and "[b]y the 1980s, there were 200 formulas and over a thousand

---

5. Long & Christensen, *supra* note *, at 115–18.

6. A recent article by Long and Christensen, *When Justices (Subconsciously) Attack: The Theory of Argumentative Threat and the Supreme Court*, 91 Oregon L. Rev. 933 (2013) more fully discusses the relationship between the use of intensifiers and readability by winning and losing brief writers and majority and dissenting judges and justices. Dissenting opinion writers use longer sentences and more intensifiers.

7. At least one excellent and easily accessible short history and explanation of readability formulas and the theory underlying them can be found on the Web. *See* William H. DuBay, *The Principles of Readability*, http://www.impact-information.com/impactinfo/ readability02.pdf (Aug. 25, 2004) (accessed Aug. 4, 2011; copy on file with Journal of Appellate Practice and Process). This paper includes an extensive bibliography of important and seminal works on readability. *See id.* at 59.

8. *Id.* at 3. DuBay also provides three additional definitions of "readability." *Id.* A less readable, but perhaps more precise, definition of readability is offered by the creator of the SMOG (Simple Measure of Gobbledegook) readability formula, G. Harry McLaughlin:

> One of the least ambiguous published definitions of readability is that given by English and English in their *Dictionary of Psychological Terms*. "Readability," they say, "is the quality of a written or printed communication that makes it easy for any given class of persons to understand its meaning, or that induces them to continue reading."

G. Harry McLaughlin, *Proposals for British Readability Measures*, in *The Third International Reading Symposium: Today's Child and Learning to Read* 186, 186 (John Downing & Amy L. Brown eds., Cassell 1968).

9. *See e.g.* DuBay, *supra* n. 7 at 2–3; Cheryl Stephens, *All About Readability*, http:// www.plainlanguagenetwork.org/stephens/readability.html (Plain Lang. Assn. Intl. 2000) (accessed Aug. 5, 2011; copy on file with Journal of Appellate Practice and Process); *see also* Jeanne S. Chall, *The Beginning Years*, in *Readability: Its Past, Present, and Future* 2, 2–4 (Beverley L. Zakulak & S. Jay Samuels eds., Intl. Reading Assn. 1988) (summarizing history of "readability measurement").

studies published on readability formulas attesting to their strong theoretical and statistical validity."[10]

Each of the hundreds of readability formulas uses a different set of semantic and syntactic factors to determine readability, but the most frequently used factors are word complexity and sentence length. And while these rather simple "surface features" exclude any consideration of content, grammar, or organization, over fifty years of research have shown that these factors are the best predictors of readability based on comprehension tests that do consider content, grammar, and organization.[11] Although almost every conceivable linguistic factor has been included in the scores of different formulas, and some formulas include a dozen or more factors, the addition of more factors does little to increase the accuracy of readability predictions and renders the formulas much more difficult to use.[12] "Put another way, counting more things does not make [a] formula any more predictive of reading ease but takes a lot more effort."[13]

Of the many readability formulas, some of the more popular and accurate formulas that rely on sentence and word length include the SMOG (Simple Measure of Gobbledegook) formula, which "measures the number of words of more than 2 syllables in a sample of 30 words,"[14] the Gunning Fog Index, which uses two variables: "in a sample of 100 words, the average number of words per sentence and the number of words of more than 2 syllables,"[15] the Flesch Reading Ease formula, which measures "the number of syllables and the number of sentences for each 100-word sample," and the Flesch-Kincaid Grade Level formula, which measures the same variables, but converts them to a grade level

---

10. *Id.* at 2. *See also* Joseph Kimble, *Answering the Critics of Plain Language*, 5 Scribes J. Leg. Writing 51 (citing numerous studies showing that plain language improves comprehension).

11. *Id.* at 35–36; *see also* Jeanne S. Chall & Edgar Dale, *Readability Revisited: The New Dale-Chall Readability Formula* 5–6 (Brookline Books 1995) ("[T]he strongest predictor of overall text difficulty [is] word difficulty.... The next best predictor of comprehension difficulty ... is sentence length. Sentence length stands up quite well as a predictor of syntactic complexity—even better than more complex syntactic measures based on sophisticated linguistic theories."). As noted *infra*, however, these claims have been questioned and criticized.

12. DuBay *supra* n. 7, at 19.

13. Stephens *supra* n. 9.

14. Geoffrey Marnell, *Measuring Readability, Part 1: The Spirit is Willing, but the Flesch is Weak* 3, http://www.abelard.com.au/readability%20statistics.pdf (accessed Aug. 15, 2011; copy on file with Journal of Appellate Practice and Process); *see also* DuBay *supra* n. 7, at 47.

15. Marnell *supra* n. 14 at 3; *see also* DuBay *supra* n. 7, at 24.

calculation.[16] Flesch Reading Ease scores range from 0 to 100; a score of 0 is practically unreadable, a score of 30 means the reading is "very difficult," a score of 70 means the reading is suitable for adult audiences, and a score of 100 means the reading is easy and should be readable by someone with a fourth grade education who is "barely 'functionally literate.'"[17]

These formulas are popular because they are relatively easy to use (all four can be applied with readily available software),[18] and they appear to be accurate because they correlate well with more sophisticated, content-based measures of reading comprehension.[19] The Flesch Reading Ease Formula is probably the most influential and popular readability formula, due in part to its adoption by Microsoft Word.

Even though readability formulas correlate with reading comprehension, this correlation has been questioned, and recently, the reliability of readability formulas has been criticized.[20] Some scholars and experts claim that readability depends more on the literacy, motivation, and background of the reader than the surface factors of the text. Some further claim that reliance on such formulas can actually decrease the readability of text, especially when "writers ... write to the formulas."[21] By trying to lower reading difficulty through the use of shorter sentences, a writer can actually reduce the semantic flow of an idea and make it more difficult to understand.

---

16. DuBay, *supra* n. 7 at 21, 50.

17. DuBay *supra* n. 7 at 21 (quoting language used by U.S. Census in 1940s); *see also* Marnell at 3 (noting that a company writing materials designed to accompany a product to be imported to the United States "was asked to ensure that the documentation had a readability score that indicated that it could be fully understood by someone with only an eighth-grade education"). Of course, the Flesch Grade Level scale approximates the reading ability of a person in a given school grade. *See e.g.* DuBay at 50.

18. Thomas Oakland & Holly B. Lane, *Language, Reading, and Readability Formulas: Implications for Developing and Adapting Tests*, 4 Intl. J. Testing 239, 250 (2004).

19. DuBay *supra* n. 7 at 22–24 (citing research), 36 (noting that "the readability variables ... with all their limitations have remained the best predictors of text difficulty as measured by comprehension tests"); McLaughlin at 191–92 (concluding that the readability measures are sufficiently predictive to be useful).

20. *See e.g.* Bertram C. Bruce, Ann D. Rubin, & Kathleen S. Starr, *Why Readability Formulas Fail* (U. of Ill. Ctr. for the Study of Reading 1981), https://www.ideals.illinois.edu.bitstream/handle/2142/15490/ why-rf-fail . pdf?sequence = 2 (criticizing readability formulas for insufficient consideration of relevant factors, lack of statistical rigor, and inappropriate use) (accessed Aug. 15, 2011; copy on file with Journal of Appellate Practice and Process).

21. Bruce *supra* n. 24 at 3 (pointing out that "[s]uch prescriptive use magnifies the inaccuracies inherent in the formulas"); *see also e.g.* Oakland & Lane at 245–50; George R. Klare, "Readability." Encyclopedia of educational research 3:1520– 1531 (The Free Press 1982).

Furthermore, predicted readability of the same text can, and usually does, vary greatly between various formulas,[22] and computerized versions of a given formula may not always faithfully execute the correct formula.[23] A particularly insightful criticism of computerized readability formulas in this regard was raised by Professor Sirico,[24] who claims that the Flesch formulas used by Microsoft Word (which are the formulas used in the Long/Christensen research) do not actually use the Flesch formulation at all, but seem to rely instead on "some algorithm to approximate the number of syllables."[25] This is why there may be discrepancies between various versions of the Flesch formulations, as well as differences between computer calculations and hand calculations of the same formula.[26]

Nevertheless, at a minimum, readability formulas can be a helpful tool for roughly gauging the difficulty of longer texts and for providing a measure for determining whether that difficulty has been reduced in the revision process.[27]

Readability formulas in legal writing have been primarily applied to statutory and contract language, ballot measures, and jury instructions, usually in an effort to comply with legislation and administrative rules requiring the use of plain language, and studies in these areas generally show that more readable language is better understood than less readable language.[28] Until recently, however, little attention has been given to the readability of legal memoranda. The common wisdom seemed to hold that readability was not applicable to the sophisticated and complex nature of legal writing.[29] While studies have

---

22. See DuBay, *supra* n. 7, at 55–56, for a discussion of this problem.

23. Sirico *supra* n. 2 at 151–52; Stockmeyer *supra* n. 20 at 47.

24. *See generally* Sirico, *supra* n. 2.

25. *Id.* at 165.

26. *Id.* at 165–66.

27. *See* Tiersma *supra* n. 4 at 225–27; Stephens, *supra* n. 9; Stockmeyer *supra* n. 24 at 47; *see also* Mary Ann Hogan, *Flesch and the Common Man: Why Foundation Bigs Should Use Little Words*, http://www.knightcommunications.org/promotion-101/news-release-workshop/flesch-and-the-common-man/ (accessed Aug. 15, 2011; copy on file with Journal of Appellate Practice and Process).

28. *See e.g.* Robert W. Benson & Joan B. Kessler, *Legalese v. Plain English: An Empirical Study of Persuasion and Credibility in Appellate Brief Writing*, 20 Loy. L.A. L. Rev. 301, 302 (1987); *see generally e.g.* Edward Fry, *The Legal Aspects of Readability*, http://www.eric.ed.gov/PDFS/ED416466.pdf (revised version of a speech given at the International Reading Association meeting in May 1989); Tiersma at 220–27; DuBay at 54–55; Robert W. Benson, *The End of Legalese: The Game is Over*, 13 N.Y. U. Rev. L. & Soc. Change 519, 547–58 (1984–85).

29. *See* James Lindgren, *Style Matters*, 92 Yale L.J. 161, 169 (1982) (characterizing Flesch's then-new *How to Write Plain English*, *supra* n. 5, as "good," but questioning the value of applying a Flesch-type analysis to legal writing and asking rhetorically: "Why force yourself

shown that plain English is preferred over legalese in legal memoranda,[30] until recently, there were no studies addressing Flesch-type readability and appellate briefs. Two recent studies that discussed readability in connection with the "Questions Presented" in appellate briefs[31] and a study of United States Supreme Court briefs and Flesch readability[32] found no correlation between Flesch readability scores of the parties' briefs and the outcome of appeal. However, to our knowledge, no other study has yet applied a regression analysis to determine whether readability of an appellate brief is related to the outcome of the appeal. The Long/Christensen study confirmed the findings of Professor Coleman and Mr. Phung and shows no relationship between the readability of a brief and the outcome of an appeal.

The Long/Christensen study database consisted of court opinions and briefs from 266 United States Supreme Court cases, 90 randomly selected state supreme court cases, and a 100 federal appellate cases. In total, the study analyzed 648 court opinions and 882 appellate briefs. Logistic regression was used to evaluate the impact of readability of the appellant and appellee briefs on the odds of reversal in the state supreme courts and the federal courts of appeals, and then again to evaluate the impact of readability of the petitioner and the respondent briefs at the Supreme Court.

The analysis indicated that the Flesch Reading Ease scores at the state and federal levels are not significantly related to outcome at the five percent significance level. The same was true for the Flesch-Kincaid Grade Level. For the analyses of the Supreme Court data, again there was no statistical evidence

---

to write at an eighth- or ninth-grade level if you are writing mainly for an audience of other lawyers?").

30. *See e.g.* Sean Flammer, An Empirical Analysis of Writing Style, Persuasion, and the Use of Plain Language, 16 Leg. Writing 183 (2010) (describing a survey showing that most state and federal judges prefer plain language over legalese and describing three earlier surveys that reached the same result); Hunter M. Breland & Frederick M. Hart, *Defining Legal Writing: An Empirical Analysis of the Legal Memorandum*, L. School Admission Council Research Rep. 93-06 (April 1994) (describing an extensive survey and regression analysis conducted to determine what constitutes good or poor legal writing); Benson & Kessler, *supra* n. 38. *Cf.* Tiersma at 211–30 (listing areas in which plain language is better understood than unduly technical language and discussing examples).

31. Judith D. Fischer, *Got Issues? An Empirical Study about Framing Them*, 6 J. Assoc. Leg. Writing Dirs. 1 (2009); Brady S. Coleman et al., *Grammatical and Structural Choices in Issue Framing: A Quantitative Analysis of "Questions Presented" from a Half Century of Supreme Court Briefs*, 29 Am. J. Tr. Advoc. 327 (2005).

32. Brady Coleman & Quy Phung, *The Language of Supreme Court Briefs: A Large-Scale Quantitative Investigation*, 11 J. App. Prac. & Process 75 (2010).

that readability or grade level had any impact on outcome. The results of the Long/Christensen study is graphically depicted in the boxplot[33] shown in Figure 1.

Figure 1. Distribution of Flesch Reading Ease for Each Writer Group

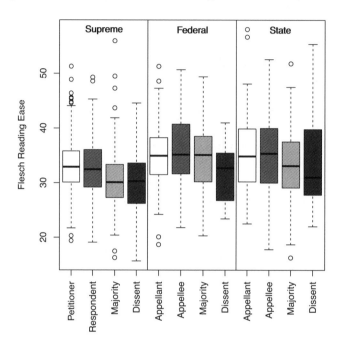

Figure 1 shows that although the means available to different writers are often significantly different, there is still a great deal of variability within each writer group.

The bottom line for legal writing students is that the Long/Christensen analysis showed no correlation between outcome on appeal and readability

---

33. A boxplot illustrates the distribution of an observed variable. The lower and upper ends of the box denote the twenty-fifth and seventy-fifth percentiles of the variable's distribution, with the line in the middle of the box denoting the median (i.e., the middle observation). The whiskers extending from the lower and upper ends of the box denote the observations in the lowest and highest quartiles of the data; the circles appearing beyond the ends of the whiskers denote unusually large or small values (which are typically referred to in statistical analysis as "outliers").

based on the Microsoft Word version of the Flesch Reading Ease scale and the Flesch-Kincaid Grade Level scale.

Even though no correlation was found between outcome and readability, there are still helpful lessons to be gleaned from the Long/Christensen study results. First, if a novice lawyer or judge wants to check whether his or her writing is near the readability level of other lawyers or judges, the novice can simply perform a Microsoft Word readability check and compare the results with our results (include your citations as part of the readability check). State court and federal appellate practitioners, judges, and justices should aim for a Reading Ease score of approximately 35 or a Grade Level score of somewhere around 13. Supreme Court practitioners should try to be a little less readable; aim for a readability score of around 33 or a Grade Level score closer to 14. New Supreme Court Justices (take note, Justices Sotomayor and Kagan) should strive for yet less readability when writing for the majority, around 30 to 31 on the Reading Ease scale and about 14.4 on the Grade Level scale. And, when writing a dissenting opinion, go for the least readable style: 29.5 on the Reading Ease scale and 15 on the Grade Level scale. Finally, in case you are wondering, this chapter earns a Reading Ease score of 30.4 and a Grade Level score of 14.1, which puts it squarely in the realm of majority-writing Supreme Court Justices. What Macbeth said about life is probably true for the impact of appellate brief readability on the outcome of an appeal: "sound and fury / Signifying nothing."[34]

Finally, nothing in the Long/Christensen study suggests that legal brief writers should not seek to write shorter, rather than longer, sentences and use shorter, rather than longer, words. Readers, including justices and judges, generally prefer concise writing and perceive "readable" writers as more credible. So, although you may gain some points with the judge, more readable writing will probably not win your appeal.

---

34. William Shakespeare, *Macbeth* act 5, sc. 5, http://shakespeare.mit.edu/macbeth/macbeth.5.5.html (accessed Aug. 23, 2011; copy of relevant page on file with Journal of Appellate Practice and Process).

Chapter 10

Narrative

Have you ever thought to begin legal analysis with "It was a dark and stormy night …"? Maybe you should. A lot of study has been given in recent years to the use of narrative, or storytelling, in writing. Different disciplines mean different things when they use the word "narrative." Journalists, for instance, use the word "narrative" to describe an article that is written in a storytelling style that describes characters of the story, demonstrates a conflict that the characters find themselves in, and then gives some sort of resolution to that conflict, instead of the traditional news story that simply describes the who, what, when, and where of the facts, organized from the most important fact to the least important fact. Creative writers often use the word narrative to describe a story that is told from one person's point of view. F. Scott Fitzgerald's *The Great Gatsby* is a famous example of a story that is told from the perspective of one character in the story—Nick Carraway.

Even lawyers can mean different things when using the word "narrative." Sometimes they mean to use the word as a synonym for "story," as in "let's tell a narrative of the Defendant's whereabouts on the night in question." And sometimes they mean the cause and effect relationship that the human mind tries to make out of otherwise disconnected experiences, as in "the Defendant's innocence is the only narrative that the jury can accept because he was 100 miles away from the crime scene when the crime happened." And sometimes attorneys use "narrative" to mean "the art of persuasion," as in "the Defense's closing argument's narrative convinced the jury of the Defendant's innocence." For purposes of this article, we will be using the term "narrative" to describe a story-telling format of writing.

Whole books have been written attempting to define the core components of a narrative, but even in its broadest definition a narrative is a description of an event or events.[1] Some scholars have other requirements for a text to be

---

1. H. Porter Abbott, THE CAMBRIDGE INTRODUCTION TO NARRATIVE, 12–13 (2008).

deemed a "narrative," like some sort of developed narrator or human characters[2] or a progression of events that demonstrate a conflict of some kind and
how that conflict is resolved.[3] For purposes of legal writing, it doesn't make
sense to spend time worrying about the mechanics of a narrative. Most of what
we deal with in law is based on the conflict of characters—clients with conflict end up in a lawyer's office—so most any narrative written about the law
will necessarily have some sort of human actors and an inherent conflict that
needs to be described. Even under the most restrictive definition of "narrative," most of the stories lawyers would want to tell meet the definition because
they involve characters that find themselves involved in some sort of conflict
and are seeking a resolution to that conflict.

There have been an increasing number of articles and legal scholarly journals that have advocated for writing in a narrative style. The theory is that the
storytelling style pulls the reader into the written word better than other possible styles of writing, and increasing the reader's attention in this manner will
benefit the reader's comprehension of the writer's message. A storytelling style
written correctly also gives the reader the satisfaction of connecting pieces of
a story into a cause-and-effect relationship. In other words, the Defendant is
innocent of the crime *because* he was 100 miles away at the time it was committed. The "because" gives the reader the satisfaction of understanding that
the fact that the Defendant was 100 miles away from the crime scene means that
the Defendant is not guilty of the crime.

The need to create causal connections that are at the heart of any narrative
is a basic tool of survival of the human brain. As one scholar described it, when
a man approaches your table at a restaurant with a pad and pen, you know
that he is a waiter who wants to take your order because you know you are in
a restaurant and have learned this cause-and-effect relationship from your previous experiences at restaurants.[4] Learning these cause-and-effect relationships
is essential to human survival so that we learn from our previous experiences.
Accordingly, the narrative cause-and-effect style fits right into that basic need
of the human brain. This sense of satisfaction for a reader makes statements
written in a narrative style particularly persuasive.

These recommendations to write legal arguments in narrative form did
not come out of thin air. There are many psychological studies that have been
conducted on narrative, or storytelling, style. And indeed it does seem that

---

2. *Id.* at 15.

3. David Herman, *Basic Elements of Narrative*, xvi (John Wiley and Sons, Ltd. 2009).

4. Steven Winter, *Legal Storytelling: The Cognitive Dimension of the Agony Between Legal Power and Narrative Meaning*, 87 MICH. L. REV. 2225 (1989).

readers pay more attention and comprehend stories better than other styles of writing. In one study fourth-graders were given two pieces of writing to read—one that was told in a traditional storytelling style and one that was told in an expository writing style, that is, the kind of style you may be used to from encyclopedias where factual information is simply described in a linear fashion without any use of characters or other narrative tools. The students were then asked to recall what they had learned about in the two written pieces. The narrative group of students could recall about 20% of what they read in the narrative documents, and of that 20%, they understood the writer's intended meaning for about 17% of the document. The expository group, on the other hand, only remembered about 10% of what they read and only took away the intended meaning of the writer on about 4% of the document.[5] Admittedly, the ability of fourth graders to learn from a written document may be much different than the ability of an adult. Even the authors of this study acknowledged that the effect of narrative on student comprehension may be affected by the comfort level that children have with a storytelling style as it is likely that children have limited exposure to expository texts in their early educational careers.

Legal scholars have conducted their own empirical studies to try and decipher whether narrative is an effective mode of legal discourse. In 2009, Kenneth Chestek, a law professor and legal writing scholar, sent "test" briefs written on a fictional case to 95 judges, law clerks, court staff attorneys, practitioners, and law professors and asked them to review the brief's persuasiveness.[6] Each reviewer received two briefs. One brief argued the case for one party using the components of a good narrative—well-developed characters who run into an obstacle and then seek to overcome that obstacle—in conjunction with setting forth the logical legal argument that supported the party's position. The second brief argued the case for the same party but only explained the logical legal argument without the accompanying narrative. Half the participants received briefs for the fictional Petitioner in the case and half received briefs for the fictional Respondent. The fact pattern was drafted in a manner so that the law favored the Petitioner's arguments and disfavored the Respondent's arguments. The majority of the reviewers found the narrative briefs more persuasive—64.2% to be exact. Additionally, Chestek found that there was no significant difference between the Petitioner and Respondent group in the evaluation of the per-

---

5. Stephen B. Kucer, *Going Beyond the Author, What Reteachings Tell us About Comprehending Narrative and Expository Texts*, Literacy, Jul 2011, Vol. 45 Issue 2, 62–69.

6. Kenneth Chestek, *Judging by the Numbers: An Empirical Study of the Power of Story*, 7 J. Ass'n Legal Writing Directors 1 (Fall 2010).

suasiveness of the narrative briefs, suggesting that whether the law is in favor of a position or not, narrative seems to have a similar persuasive effect.

Despite all of this positive news on the power of writing in a narrative style, there do appear to be some limitations to the narrative style of writing. Michael Dahlstrum, a professor in the School of Journalism at Iowa State University, conducted a study that looked at the recall 92 undergraduates had of information in passages that incorporated various fake environmental messages. Dahlstrum discovered that when the messages were an integral part of the story that caused the main character to act in a certain way, the undergraduates not only recalled the information more readily but also perceived it to be true more often than environmental messages that were, essentially, side notes to the story that did not cause the main character to act in a particular manner. It follows that a persuasive narrative incorporates the message of the narrative as part of the cause-and-effect storyline of the narrative. If the writer simply throws the point in as a side note to the story and doesn't link it to the main character's development in the story through a cause-and-effect relationship, the point will likely be lost on the reader.

So what does all this mean for your legal writing? The empirical studies support the concept that well-drafted narrative stories can better reader comprehension of a point you are trying to convey and can convince the reader that the point you are conveying is true to a greater degree than simply stating the point. To be well-drafted, the point of the narrative must be worked into the story in a way that shows a clear cause-and-effect relationship on the characters involved in the story. This certainly makes narrative an easy choice for descriptions of facts in legal writing, especially when explaining those facts in a persuasive manner. And if there is a way to draft your analysis of the law in a narrative format that incorporates your analysis in a clear cause-and-effect relationship, then using a narrative description makes sense as well. However, if it is impossible to work the legal points into the narrative's cause-and-effect relationship, narrative may not be as worthwhile of a choice.

Chapter 11

Macro-Organization of Legal Analysis

Besides the inevitability of repaying student loans, if there is one thing law students have universally learned, it is the mnemonic device of IRAC or CREAC. Mnemonics for legal organization may take many forms, but they generally follow the same basic structure.[1] That structure, regardless of how complicated the mnemonic gets, remains simple. Legal reasoning and argument takes the form of a deductive syllogism.[2]

Almost all legal writing texts, with the notable exception of the Dernbach text,[3] proffer some version of CREAC, explain how it is based on a deductive syllogism, and make some claim as to why this organization is preferred. Here are some examples of CREAC formulations:

CRAC, CIRAC,[4] IEAPC,[5] CRRPAP,[6] CRuPAC[7]

Our favorite is, of course, TREAT, the formulation created by Murray and DeSanctis.[8] Not because we think it is necessarily a superior formulation of CREAC, but because it sounds like it might actually be tasty. Most other legal

---

1. Christine Coughlin et al., *A Lawyer Writes* 82–83 (2008).

2. *See generally* Charles R. Calleros, Legal Method and Writing 68–72 (5th ed. 2006); Mary Beth Beazley, A Practice Guide to Appellate Advocacy 61–63 (2nd ed. 2006).

3. John C. Dernbach et al., *A Practical Guide to Legal Writing and Legal Method* (4th ed. 2010).

4. Nancy L. Schultz & Louis J. Sirico, Jr., *Legal Writing and Other Lawyering Skills* 42 (5th ed. 2010).

5. Helene S. Shapo et al., *Writing and Analysis in the Law* 207–08, 143 (5th ed. 2008) (The authors do not explicitly articulate this mnemonic formulation, but it follows from their articulation of the order of analysis).

6. Christine Coughlin et al., *A Lawyer Writes: A Practical Guide to Legal Analysis* 83 (2008).

7. Richard K. Neumann, Jr., *Legal Reasoning and Legal Writing: Structure, Strategy, and Style* 101 (5th ed. 2005).

8. Michael D. Murray & Christy H. DeSanctis, *Legal Writing and Analysis* 20 (2d ed., 2009).

writing texts offer similar instruction even if no specific acronym or mnemonic device is articulated.[9]

So, is syllogistic reasoning the best way to make a legal argument? And if so, what evidence supports such a claim? The support for syllogistic reasoning, per se, in legal writing is treated in Chapter 5, but this Chapter asks why syllogistic reasoning in legal writing is organized in a CREAC fashion instead of a strict syllogistic fashion. Is CREAC really the best organization for a legal argument? What evidence supports that claim?

The meaning of the CREAC acronym is, generally, as follows:

C = Conclusion

R = Rule

E = Rule Explanation

A = Rule Application

C = Conclusion

On the other hand, a traditional syllogism looks something like this:

Major premise:	All humans are mortal
Minor premise:	Socrates is human
Conclusion:	Therefore, Socrates is mortal[10]

Applied to a CREAC organization, the syllogistic structure is altered. In CREAC, the major premise is the rule, the minor premise is the application of a set of facts to the rule, and the conclusion is the "resolution of the question whether the facts stated in the minor premise satisfy the legal standard stated in the major premise."[11]

In other words, if a strict syllogistic structure were used, CREAC would look like this:

R = Major premise/Rule Explanation

A = Minor premise/Rule Application

C = Conclusion/Conclusion

---

9. *See, e.g.*, Linda H. Edwards, *Legal Writing and Analysis* 91 (2003).
10. Calleros, *Legal Method and Writing*, *Supra* note 2, at 68–69.
11. *Id.*

The initial conclusion "C" and the rule explanation "E" are left out. Of course, the major premise could also be considered as the "E," but then the "R" would be left out.

As for why lawyers use this format over any other, the authors of the various texts of legal writing do not consider any alternative organizational schemes. While some texts note that inductive reasoning methods may be acceptable in the planning and pre-drafting phases of a legal memo, it is claimed that to use anything but the deductive method would end up confusing a reader.[12] This confusion, or lack of it with deduction, is because the syllogism is how the reader expects the information to be presented.[13]

This explanation, however, leads to a problem of circularity: senior attorneys and judges expect junior associates and students to use the deductive organizational scheme because that is what they are familiar with, and that is what they are familiar with because that is what was expected of them by their superiors when they were junior associates and students.

Returning to the question asked at the beginning of this Chapter, what evidence is there that the CREAC formulation of deductive reasoning is the "best" organization for legal reasoning? A few legal writing texts have articulated some reasons. For example, Richard Neumann suggests that the conclusion should precede the rule of a formal syllogism because, "a practical and busy reader needs to know what you are trying to support before you start supporting it. If your conclusion is mentioned for the first time *after* the analysis that supports it ... some or all your reasoning seems pointless to the reader who does not yet know what your reasoning is supposed to prove."[14]

Neumann similarly suggests that the skeptical reader will immediately want to know the rule of law that leads to the conclusion stated, and that the same reader will not believe that the rule is "really" the rule until it is adequately explained and "has been proved with authority."[15] As for why the rule application follows the rule explanation, Neumann pragmatically states that the application is placed last "because that is the only thing left."

In the same spirit, Robin Wellford Slocum's text states, "The deductive writing pattern is premised on the notion that readers can absorb information more easily if they understand its significance as soon as they see it. The best

---

12. Robin Wellford Slocum, *Legal Reasoning, Writing, and Other Lawyering Skills* 156 (3rd ed. 2011).

13. *Id.* at 158.

14. Richard K. Neumann, Jr., *Legal Reasoning and Legal Writing: Structure, Strategy, and Style* 103 (5th ed. 2005).

15. *Id.*

way to assure immediate understanding is to present the context of an idea before describing its details."[16]

As noted in Chapter 5, there is a certain resemblance between the arithmetic property of transitivity and syllogistic reasoning, and studies have shown that at a young age children acquire the ability to think deductively.[17] We tend to lose this ability as we get older.[18] We are not aware of any empirical study or survey that concludes that legal thinkers prefer CREAC to any other formulation of legal reasoning. Nor are we aware of any research suggesting that one is more likely to win a motion of appeal if the arguments are organized according to the CREAC method.

While the legal literature and the general literature of argumentation theory is "immense," as noted by Paul Wangerin, "much of the literature in the field has little or nothing to do with the *structure* of persuasive arguments."[19] Further summarizing the state of the research, Wangerin states that the most that can be gleaned from the existing studies is that "different audiences respond differently to different types of arguments."[20] Although this statement is most likely true, it is not exactly helpful guidance to the novice legal writer. More helpful is his summary of research on *ideas* related to the structure of legal arguments:

> [R]esearchers have discovered, among other things, that audiences tend to think that people who make organized arguments are more credible than people who make disorganized arguments. Also, as noted above, credible people tend to be more persuasive than noncredible people. Research on the differences between organized and disorganized arguments has also revealed that audiences tend to have certain relatively clear expectations regarding the organization or structure of arguments. Thus, researchers in this field now think that audiences react more favorably to arguments that are organized in familiar forms than to arguments that are organized in unfamiliar forms.[21]

---

16. Robin Wellford Slocum, *Legal Reasoning, Writing, and Other Lawyering Skills* 156 (3d ed. 2011).

17. Bruno G. Bara & Monica Bucciarelli, *Development of Syllogistic Reasoning* 157–158 Am. J. of Psychol., Vol. 108, No. 2, (Summer 1995).

18. Wim De Neys & Elke Van Gelder, *Logic and Belief Across the Lifespan: The Rise and Fall of Belief Inhibition During Syllogistic Reasoning* 123–124 Developmental Science 12:1 (2009).

19. Paul T. Wangerin, *A Multidisciplinary Analysis of the Structure of Persuasive Arguments,* 16 Har. J. L. & Pub. Pol'y 199 (1993).

20. *Id.* at 200.

21. *Id.* at 201 (footnotes omitted).

Finally, Neumann's advice about putting a conclusion first is supported by Wangerin's assertion that research tends to show that arguments placed at the beginning of a message are more persuasive than those placed elsewhere.[22]

Therefore, although there is a lack of specific research treating the efficacy and persuasiveness of CREAC specifically, the related research suggests that since CREAC is a familiar form and an organized (as opposed to unorganized) form of argument, it will likely be more persuasive than an alternative form. The takeaway for legal writers is that it is probably best to stick with the form of syllogistic reasoning found in a CREAC-type formulation. At the very least, it will be familiar to your reader and therefore more easily followed, and hopefully more persuasive.

---

22. *Id.* at 201–02.

Chapter 12

Introductions, Transitions, and Conclusions

Do readers like to be given an overview of a legal analysis before you tell the reader about the analysis, only to be reminded about a summary of the analysis afterwords? You betcha! Studies have shown that one of the greatest efforts you can make in your writing to increase reader comprehension is to give your reader a sense of organization to the material you are presenting. Legal writing books uniformly recommend that new legal writers embrace the idea of including introductions to their writing to give the reader a broad overview of where a document is going. These books also suggest using transitions to link the concepts you present in a document and writing formal conclusions that summarize where the document has been. Without a doubt, this emphasis on demonstrating a structure for the reader is supported by the studies of cognitive psychologists conducted in the '60s, '70s, and '80s that showed these structural components can have a positive effect on learning and reader comprehension. This chapter will explain these studies to you and suggest that the use of these organizational tools is a necessary component of quality legal writing.

Introductions

In 1960, a New York psychiatrist and cognitive learning theorist by the name of David Ausubel published an article titled "The use of advance organizers in the learning and retention of meaningful verbal material" in the Journal of Educational Psychology.[1] In it, Dr. Ausubel postulated that teachers that began lessons with an overview of where the lesson would take the students would find the students had a higher retention rate of the material being taught. Dr.

---

1. David P. Ausubel, *The Use of Advance Organizers in the Learning and Retention of Meaningful Verbal Material*, 51(5), J. of Educ. Psychol. 267, 272 (Oct. 1960).

Ausubel suggested that teachers start lessons with an overview of material that will be covered and a roadmap of the structure of the lesson. This introduction to the lesson, Dr. Ausubel postulated, would allow students to make connections between information they already know and the new information that was about to be presented to them. Teachers that used this introductory method to lessons were termed "advanced organizers" because the teachers gave the students an advanced idea of the organization and material that would be covered in the lesson the students were about to receive.

Dr. Ausubel's theories must have captured the interest of a large number of academics because by the late 1970s hundreds of academic studies had been conducted to determine whether "advanced organizers" had any actual effect on the learning that was occurring in classrooms. These studies received mixed results. So in 1979, John Luiten examined the studies[2] to try to make sense of the varying results. What he found was that many of the studies had flaws. For example, some had correlated statistics incorrectly; some had sample sizes that were too small. And when Luiten corrected for these errors he discovered that there was a statistically significant increase in learning that took place in classrooms where advanced organizers applied Ausubelian introductions to the lessons given to students.

Luiten found in one study he reviewed that the average student who learned from an advanced organizer learned more material than 75% of the students who did not learn from an advanced organizer. Luiten found 58% of the students in another study learned more material from an advanced organizer. However, what was most striking about the Lutein study of the studies on advanced organizers was that the retention rate of the information was much greater over time for the students who learned from advanced organizers than the students who didn't. Luiten's study also demonstrated that college-aged students had the greatest learning gains due to advanced organizers as compared to younger students, and students learning about the social sciences had the greatest learning gains due to advanced organizers as compared to students learning about mathematics or traditional sciences, like biology and physics.

You may notice that the very audience that legal writing tends to be directed at—adult learners learning about a social science—is the audience that the Lutein study indicated benefits the most from having an overview of a lesson before a teacher launches into the lesson. Indeed, legal writers are very much like teachers. Legal writers teach legal readers about a specific area of the law and how that law applies to a specific set of facts. It correlates that using the Ausebelian principles of advanced organizers will assist legal readers in learn-

2. John Luiten and Others, *The Advanced Organizer: a Review of Research Using Glass's Technique of Meta-Analysis*, (1979) http://files.eric.edu/gov/fulltext/ED171803.pdf.

ing and retaining the information the legal writer wants to convey. Perhaps that is why every legal writing textbook we reviewed focused on introductions as a powerful tool in the legal writer's toolbox.

The major legal writing textbooks impress upon new legal writers that the introduction should do two main things—introduce the reader to the legal issues that will be covered and give the reader an idea of the manner in which those issues will be discussed. This may seem very similar to the Ausubelian principles of giving students an overview of the material to be taught and the manner in which that material will be conveyed. This similarity is not coincidence. These principles do make for better learning and retention according to the Lutein study.

There is some specific information legal writers often know that can give the legal "learner" an idea of the legal issues that will be covered in a document and the manner in which they will be covered. First, the legal writer can offer the legal learner a summary of the law and how that law applies to the facts, including the ultimate conclusion the legal reader may make on what a court will decide on a certain set of facts. Of course this summary must be brief for it to be an effective overview of the document and should be presented in a manner that indicates the order it will be presented in the document so that the reader can understand the manner in which the information will be "taught." Additionally, there is often background information a legal reader needs to know before the legal writer begins the overview of the law. Presenting this information to the reader in the introductory paragraph not only makes practical sense, but also fits with the Ausbelian principle that students use the overview to make connections between the knowledge they already have and the knowledge they are about to acquire.

Transitions

If advanced organizers give legal learners an idea of the structure of the "lesson" that is before them, transitions are the scaffolding that holds that structure together. Transitions come in all shapes and sizes, but all of them do the same thing. They move the reader's focus from one thing to another. At the sentence level, a transition can be as simple as one word, like "however," that links the ideas of one sentence to the ideas of another. At the paragraph level, an effective transition might indicate to the reader that this paragraph will be discussing a new idea: "Unlike the plaintiff in the Smith case, Mr. Jones is not related to the testator ..." At the document level, informative headings often help a reader transition from one section to another. All of these transitions have one thing in common—they signal the reader that something new they are about to learn connects with something they already know in a particular way. And this connection is the one that Dr. Ausubel and the cognitive theorists that have come after him have indicated assist learners in acquiring new information.

Transitions of substantive value have been studied with mixed results. Headings that give the reader the idea of the information contained in that section have been shown in some studies to benefit comprehension,[3] especially when those headings are organized around meaningful concepts for the learning that is taking place. For example, one study looked at organizing textbooks around conceptually meaningful concepts, like a history book that is broken out into concepts like "French Geography," "French Military." These conceptually meaningful organized textbooks were compared to textbooks that organized material in grouping of less meaningful conceptual relevance for learners, such as the temporal grouping of "France—1800–1810."[4]

That study found that the meaningful conceptual headings did seem to have an effect on the student's understanding those concepts versus the temporal organization. There is, at least, one study that showed that headings had no effect at all on comprehension of a product warranty, although the study did suggest that readers preferred reading a warranty that did divide up the sections by headings,[5] but the majority of studies on headings do show a positive effect on comprehension when headings appropriately captured the material that the reader was supposed to learn from the document.

Transitions that link new concepts to old concepts by repeating words between two sentences have mostly been studied as tools of a document's "cohesion."[6] Here's an example of this kind of cohesion: "As I was driving, I saw a dog running down the street. The running dog darted in and out of cars." Using the repeated words "running dog" in the second sentence is a marker that indicates to the reader that the second sentence adds more information to the information the reader learned in the first sentence. Morton Ann Gernsbacher has conducted many of the studies on cohesion as it relates to transitions between sentences.[7] Based on her research, she theorizes that cognitive processes work much like papier-mâché. Learners, or legal readers in the case

---

3. Daniel Felkner and others, Guidelines for Document Designers, National Institute of Education, Nov. 1981, http://eric.ed.gov/ERICWebPortal/contentdelivery/servlet/ERIC-Servlet?accno=ED221866.

4. Kulhavy, R., Schmid, r. & Walker, C., *Temporal organization in prose.* AMERICAN EDUCATIONAL RESEARCH JOURNAL, 1977, 14, 115–123.

5. Supra, note 2.

6. Morton Ann Gernsbacher, *Coherence Cues Mapping During Comprehension*, in *Processing Interclausal Relationships: Studies in the Production and Comprehension of Text*, 1 (Jean Costermans & Michel Fayol eds., Lawrence Erlbaum Associates 1997).

7. *Id.*

of legal writing, start off with a beginning structure for the information they are about to receive. Then, the paper is glued on the structure through the use of transitory language that indicates to the reader exactly where the paper should be laid. These sorts of linkages between sentences, or transitions, help the reader understand that structure.

Another common type of transition used by legal writers is referred to in the social science literature as "connectives." Words like "however," "therefore," "and," "so," and "because" are all examples of connectives. Connectives do nothing more than indicate a causal connection between clauses. The research on connectives has been mixed.[8] Several studies have found that the use of connectives speeds up reading and helps readers recall the information in the second clause or sentence that is connected by the connective.

However, there have been several studies conducted that found otherwise. One in particular was conducted by Jonathan Golding and his colleagues at the University of Kentucky. Golding gave college students two sentences to read on a computer. Some students received sentences that were linked with a connective and some were not. The computer monitored the time it took the students to read the two sentences. Golding found that when the sentences were rather clearly connected without the connective, the use of a connective actually slowed down the reading time. When the sentences were not clearly related, the connective sped up the reading time. Additionally, Golding found that the use of a connective did not make a significant difference in the amount of recall of the material presented in the two clauses. Although the conclusions of these studies are mixed, it does appear that connectives can assist readers in seeing connections that are not readily apparent.

Conclusions

Conclusions added at the end of documents have not been studied in any particular depth in relation to reading comprehension. However, conclusions have a strong persuasive value that can be beneficial even for documents that are not designed to be persuasive. One of the most studied aspects of persuasion is repetition. The bulk of repetition studies have been conducted in the field of advertising, but their conclusions can be easily extrapolated to legal

---

8. Jonathan M. Golding et. al., *The Effect of Connectives and Causal Relatedness on Text Comprehension*, in *Sources of Coherence in Reading*, 127 (Robert F. Lorch Jr. & Edward J. O'Brien eds., Lawrence Erlbaum Associates. 1995).

writing. These studies conclude that repetition is good for persuasion.[9] The more exposure someone gets to a concept, the more that person will like that concept.

The father of repetition research is Robert Zajonc. He wrote an article in 1968 where he compiled a body of research that indicated that mere repetition could create a positive affinity between a person and the thing the person has been exposed to.[10] Zajonc was spurred to study the effect of repetition after reading an article about a professor at Oregon State University who had a student attend a class in a black bag. The students in the class, at first, reacted with hostility towards the student in the black bag, but eventually became friendly with the student in the black bag. Zajonc postulated that this friendly attitude came from the repeat exposure to the student in the black bag, and Zajonc supported this theory by compiling a body of research that indicated that mere repetition breeds affinity for a concept.

One of the most compelling experiments Zajonc cited involved nonsense words that college students were taught to pronounce. The students were told the nonsense words were Turkish adjectives. The students where then given a list of the nonsense words they had learned to pronounce mixed in with other nonsense words and asked to indicate whether they thought the words were good or bad adjectives. The student consistently rated words they had pronounced as having a better connotation than those they had no familiarity with.[11]

If repeat exposure to a concept breeds affinity in a test subject, it stands to reason that writing a formal conclusion in a document that summarizes the same conclusions made in the main body of the document must breed some sort of affinity with those conclusions. While this is a persuasive technique that could be used to "sell" a court on a legal argument, it is also a technique that can be used to "sell" any reader on an objective conclusion as well. So although in legal writing we generally think persuasion is a creature of advocacy-driven documents, like briefs to a court, this sort of persuasive tool can be used effectively in an objective piece to make a reader fully realize the conclusion the document is supporting.

---

9. Alan Sawyer, Repetition, Cognitive Responses, and Persuasion, Chapter 11 in Cognitive Responses in Repetition, Edited by RICHARD E. PETTY University of Missouri-Columbia THOMAS M. OSTROM TIMOTHY C. BROCK, LAWRENCE ERLBAUM ASSOCIATES, PUBLISHERS 1981 Hillsdale, New Jersey.

10. Robert Zajonc, *Attitudinal effects of Mere Exposure*, 9 J. OF PERSONALITY & SOCIAL PSYCHOL. MONOGRAPH SUPP., June 1968.

11. *Id.* 13–14.

Introductions, Transitions, and Conclusions Exercise

Now that you know the benefits of introductions, transitions, and conclusions, let's assess some. Assuming you were writing a document that analyzed if a defendant could be charged with false imprisonment for being detained on suspicion of shoplifting by store employees, which introduction would you find the most helpful and why?

I.

Intro. 1:

A customer may have a claim for false imprisonment if a store official improperly detains him to determine if the customer had been shoplifting. The Florida false imprisonment statute permits a merchant to detain a customer in a reasonable manner and for a reasonable length of time, if he or she has probable cause to believe that the customer has committed a theft, and that he or she can recover the property by taking the customer into custody. Fla. Stat. § 812.015 (3)(a) (West 2000). To avoid liability, the merchant detaining the suspect must (a) have probable cause to believe the merchandise has been taken; (b) detain the suspect in a reasonable manner for a reasonable time; and (c) call a peace officer to the scene immediately after the suspect is taken into custody. *Weismann v. K-Mart Corp.*, 396 So. 2d 1164, 1166 (Fla. Ct. Dist. App. 1981). Because Mr. Weiderman was only held for a short period of time while the store called police, and it did appear as if Mr. Weiderman put the necklace in his pants pocket, a court will likely not find the store liable for false imprisonment.

Intro. 2:

Stores can be held liable for false imprisonment when they hold someone unlawfully. *Weismann v. K-Mart Corp.*, 396 So. 2d 1164, 1166 (Fla. 3d Dist. App. 1981). The store did not hold Mr. Weiderman unlawfully because it did look like he stole the necklace and stores have a right to try and recover stolen merchandise. Also, the store was quick to release Weiderman when it was discovered that he didn't steal the necklace.

II.

Now, let's think a little about transitions. Which passage do you prefer and why?

Passage 1:

The store will likely argue that it had reasonable cause to detain Weiderman for the entire time he was detained. Initially, a store employee noticed a necklace missing immediately after seeing Weiderman suddenly reach into his pocket.

These two facts gave the store employee reasonable cause to detain Weiderman. The reasonable cause continued while the manager searched the area near where the necklace was and found it. Once the manager found the necklace, the reasonable cause expired, but Weiderman was released at that time.

Passage 2:

The store will argue that the length of the detention was reasonable because the employee had reasonable cause to detain Weiderman at all times during the detention. The store will argue that its employee had reasonable cause to initially detain Gerwin when he noticed that a necklace was missing after observing Gerwin suddenly reach into his pocket. The store will also argue that reasonable cause for Gerwin's detention continued until the manager completed the search.

III.

Finally, let's take a look at some conclusion for this piece. Which conclusion do you think is most effective and why?

Conclusion 1:

Under Florida law, Weiderman will not likely have a claim for false imprisonment against the store. To state a false imprisonment claim against a merchant, the customer must prove that the detention was unreasonable. Weiderman cannot prove false imprisonment.

Conclusion 2:

Under Florida law, Weiderman will not likely have a claim for false imprisonment against the bookstore. To state a false imprisonment claim against a merchant, the customer must prove that there was no probable cause for his detention or that he was held for an unreasonable length of time. Because the employee saw Weiderman put his hand in his pocket right before noticing the necklace was gone, the employee had reasonable cause to detain Weiderman and Weiderman was only held long enough for the manager to look and find the necklace.

Chapter 13

Micro-Organization of Legal Analysis

Now that we've taken a look at the legal writing conventions regarding macro-organization and the empirical studies that support those, as well as the structural tools for macro-organization (introductions, transitions, and conclusions), the time has come to look at the micro-organization of legal analysis. Many of the same concepts that apply to the macro-organization of a legal document apply on the micro-organization, or paragraph level, of the document as well. Luckily for those of us who study and analyze the law, there is a rhythm to law that allows legal writers to use a somewhat formulaic approach to writing at the sentence level.

Although every legal analysis will involve different law and different facts, legal writers, generally, are tasked with explaining to the reader how the facts of a legal problem will likely be analyzed in light of precedent cases. This recursive nature of legal analysis sets forth a somewhat predictable hierarchy of information for the reader. The reader needs to understand the law before applying that law to a new set of facts. And helping the reader understand the overarching point of the analysis is helpful for comprehension and retention as we learned in the chapter on introductions and conclusions.

From these generalities, legal writers have been able to develop a lexicon of acronyms that help legal writers remember the various components of legal analysis and the order in which those components should be explained. You may remember from Chapter 11 that these acronyms work well for macro-organization. They also work well for the micro-organization of legal analysis. The empirical studies conducted on the paragraph level of writing support the same formulaic approach to paragraphs as legal writers tend to follow for an entire legal document—because of the nature of legal analysis, paragraphs describing the law and applying the law to the facts tend to be best written when the main point of the paragraph is stated at the beginning and the end of the paragraph (the "C"), the rule that is applied in the paragraph is explained (the "R"), and then applied to the material explained in the paragraph (the "A"). Most of all of the acronyms used for macro-organization follow this pattern, although they may use different terms.

Since the mid-1800s,[1] writers have been instructed to endeavor to start paragraphs with a topic sentence, that is, a sentence that summarizes the main point of the paragraph. Research that was conducted in the latter half of the 20th century finally demonstrated support for the heralded topic sentence. In two studies conducted in the mid-1970s, researchers determined that study participants comprehended information better and retained it longer if the information was explained in paragraphs that began with topic sentences.[2] Further studies have shown that there is a reader expectation that the first sentence in a paragraph is the topic sentence, and that the reader further identifies the topic sentence by reading the other sentences in the paragraph and verifying that the topic sentence does, indeed, describe the main meaning of the paragraph.[3]

If readers process and retain information better with topic sentences, and readers expect topic sentences to be located at the beginning of a paragraph and summarize the main point of the paragraph, the first sentence of most paragraphs in a legal writing document should start with a topic sentence that summarizes the point of that paragraph. In law, there are particularized goals of most paragraphs. Most paragraphs in a legal writing document are either describing law or applying that law to a new set of facts. Describing those goals in a topic sentence of a paragraph, then, should be an effective way of demonstrating the main point of the paragraph. For a paragraph that describes the law, that goal is, generally, to inform the reader of the main rule, or rules, of law that the reader should understand from reading about that law.

More specifically, if a paragraph describes a particular case, the best topic sentence is usually the rule from the case that the reader needs to understand because it will be applied to the facts later on when the writer analyzes how the law applies to the facts at issue. If a paragraph describes how the law applies to the facts at issue, a topic sentence could summarize the main point of that paragraph—that might be an argument you think a party might make or a decision you think a court might make—depending on the nature of the document and your analysis.

---

1. Mike Duncan, Whatever Happened to the Paragraph, 69:5 College English 470 (2007).

2. M.W. Aulls, M. W. (1975). Expository paragraph properties that influence literal recall, Journal of Reading Behavior, 7, 391–399.; David Keiras, Good and bad structure in simple paragraphs: Effects on apparent theme, reading time, and recall. Detail Only Available Kieras, David E.; Journal of Verbal Learning & Verbal Behavior, Vol 17(1), Feb, 1978. pp. 13–28.

3. Philip M. McCarthy, et. al, Identifying Topic Sentencehood, 40:3 Behavior Research Methods 647–664 (2008).

The other sentences in a paragraph do their job more effectively if they proceed in a fashion that allows readers to see the linear connections between sentences.[4] Researchers at the Carnegie-Mellon Computerized Psychology Laboratory looked at how readers process sentences in a paragraph in a study conducted on a group of 35 students and staff of Carnegie Mellon University. The researchers gave the students 20 passages that contained simple sentences describing ants eating jelly on a kitchen counter. When placed in the right order, the sentences each referenced an idea or concept that had already been introduced to the reader in a previous sentence. When placed in a different order, sentences referred to ideas or concepts that had not been introduced to the reader yet.

The researchers found that the subjects of the study were more adept at identifying the main point of the paragraph if sentences progressed in a manner that allowed each sentence to reference an idea or concept that had already been introduced to the reader in a previous sentence. The researchers hypothesized that the reason for this phenomenon can be found in the short-term memory processes of the subjects. As the theory goes, every time a reader is introduced to new information, the reader stores that concept as a "chunk" of information in the reader's brain. The more information being stored in short-term memory, the more time it takes a reader to retrieve individual "chunks" of information, which slows down reading time and makes deciphering the main point of the paragraph more difficult. However, if the connections between "chunks" is demonstrated for the reader, retrieval of that information is much faster.

Therefore, the researchers postulate, that the empirical research discovered in this study indicates that the best sentence structure for comprehension is organizing sentences in a sequential order that allows each new sentence to refer to some information that was covered in a proceeding sentence. This process of referring to information in previous sentences is sometimes called the "given-new" process of sentence organization within a paragraph.

Based on what we know about the given-new process of sentence organization, there are some writing generalizations that follow in most legal writing situations. Explaining the law, especially when cases are involved, can only be organized in a few ways to achieve the given-new sequential order of sentence organization. Generally, there is no way to explain the rule a court used to reach its conclusion, the reasoning the court used to reach its conclusions or

---

4. David E. Keiras, Good and Bad Structure in Simple Paragraphs, 17 *Journal of Verbal Learning and Verbal Behavior* 13–28 (1978).

the outcome of a court opinion without first describing the facts of the case. Once the facts are described, many of the subsequent sentences will have references to previous information in the paragraph because many sentences in a paragraph about a case describe how the court analyzed the facts of the case.

Although certainly not impossible, it is hard to imagine how the facts can be described after the rule of law or reasoning of a case without the rule and reasoning sentences referring to the facts before the facts are fully explained. Additionally, because the reasoning the court uses to get to its conclusion usually discusses the facts and the rule of law the court is applying to the facts, it makes sense to explain the facts and the rule of law before the reasoning of the court. Finally, because the conclusion of the court is generally arrived at after a court reasons through the rule of law and how it applies to the facts, the only way to follow a given-new structure is to make sure the conclusion comes at the end of the explanation of the case.

At this point, you may notice that this generalized organization for a paragraph that explains a case seems to mimic the macro-organization acronyms that legal writers have developed to act as a guide for organization of most legal analysis. If the topic sentence of a paragraph that explains a case focuses on the main point of the paragraph and the main point of the paragraph is the conclusion the court comes to, then the topic sentence is, in essence, a "conclusion" (the first "C" in CRAC). If the writer then explains the facts of the case, then the rule used by the court in the case (the "R" in CRAC), then the analysis the court uses to decide how the rule applies to those facts (the "A" in CRAC), and then the conclusion the court arrives at (the last "C" in CRAC) then the explanation of the case does follow a similar CRAC pattern.

Certainly, there are times when an explanation of a case cannot fit into this mold. One of the most frequent is if the purpose of explaining a case is for something other than the case's outcome. In those instances the "C" in the topic sentence that focuses on the main point the reader should get out of the case and the "C" at the end of the paragraph may not match. It is for this reason that being wed to an acronym like "CRAC," without understanding the reasons behind it, can be frustrating for a legal writer. If the legal writer knows why the acronym generally works, the writer can assess if the acronym is not working for a good reason.

Following the given-new approach in paragraphs that focus on the writer's personal assessment of how the law applies to the facts is a much harder paragraph structure to predict because there is no standard set of information that will be covered in one of these paragraphs. Depending on the purpose of the legal document and the ways in which the individual law pertains to the legal issue and the specific facts of the case, these sorts of paragraphs could be attempting to make any number of points to a reader. These types of paragraphs could be summarizing an argument that the writer thinks a party might make to a court as to how the law applies to the facts. These types of paragraphs could be explaining how social policy might cause a court to side with a weaker argument in order to resolve the dispute that is fair to both parties.

But, despite the unpredictability of these types of paragraphs, a legal writer can be guided by what we know about good organization on the paragraph level—beginning the paragraph with a topic sentence that gives the reader the main point of the paragraph and organizing sentences in a manner that takes advantage of the given-new structure will be the most effective organization for a reader.

Micro-Organization Exercise

Let's take a look at a couple of paragraphs that describe a case. Which one do you like better and why?

Paragraph 1:

The length of a detention is reasonable if the merchant has reasonable cause to detain the customer at all times during the detention. Canto v. Ivey & Co., 595 So. 2d 1025, 1027 (Fla. 1st Dist. App. 1992). In Canto, the store's security camera showed a child at a display table handing something to another child, which the child placed in his pocket. *Id. at 1027.* Subsequently, a store employee apprehended the two children for shoplifting when they were leaving the store. *Id.* The employee detained the children for two hours until an officer arrived at the store. *Id.* The officer released the children after he completed the search and found no merchandise on them. *Id.* The court concluded that the detention was reasonable in length because after viewing the security camera the store employee had reasonable cause to initially detain the children. *Id. at 1027.* The court further reasoned that because the store employee thought it was improper to search the children and decided to call the police, reasonable cause for the detention continued until the search was completed. *Id.*

Paragraph 2:

In Canto v. Ivey, the court reasoned that a detention was reasonable in length because after viewing the security camera the store employee had reasonable cause to initially detain the children. Canto v. Ivey & Co., 595 So. 2d 1025, 1027 (Fla. 1st Dist. App. 1992). The court further reasoned that because the store employee thought it was improper to search the children and decided to call the police, reasonable cause for the detention continued until the search was completed. *Id.* The store's security camera showed a child at a display table handing something to another child, which the child placed in his pocket. *Id.* at 1027. Subsequently, a store employee apprehended the two children for shoplifting when they were leaving the store. *Id.* The employee detained the children for two hours until an officer arrived at the store. *Id.* The officer released the children after he completed the search and found no merchandise on them. *Id.*

Chapter 14

Citation—Does Anybody Really Care?

New law students are often shocked by the amount of attribution that takes place in a legal writing document. This shock, no doubt, comes from the fact that the amount of citation in legal documents is much more extensive than citation found in any other genre of writing. Certainly, formatting citations is a lengthy process that can sometimes aggravate new writers because of the time involved in what seems like a rather simple piece of information. So the students' reactions to the amount of citations in legal documents may be somewhat due to the fear involved in learning how to write citations. While there may be some debate regarding the proper role of citations in legal analysis, one thing is clear—culturally, lawyers cite frequently and judges expect a high level of citation in cases coming before the court.

As many scholars have pointed out, there are striking inconsistencies between the theory and the practice of attribution. For instance, students new to attribution are often told that any thought that they take from someone else should be attributed. In fact, the ALWD citation manual indicates in rule 34.2 that a writer should include a citation any time a sentence references a "description of the legal authority, or an idea, a thought, an expression borrowed from another source." However, there are multitudes of situations where that theory doesn't hold true. In law, one of the most frequent situations is when a law clerk drafts documents for a judge or an associate drafts a document for a partner. The associate and the law clerk often draft the entire document, but their name appears nowhere on it when the document arrives at its intended audience. Additionally, lawyers often look to "model" documents created by other lawyers when drafting documents the lawyer may be unfamiliar with. These lawyers often use the language of the model document verbatim when drafting their document and do not attribute to that model document at all.

The empirical research seems to indicate that this inconsistency is due to the customary nature of citation.[1] It appears that there are just some situations where readers do not expect citation because the reader understands through other means that the idea expressed in the document has a source other than the writer and does not need that explained in an explicit format.

In a study conducted by a researcher from the linguistic department at Columbia University, test subjects were asked to review a passage where an author explicitly attributed an argument supporting funding for public transportation to another source. The passage also included another argument for public transportation funding that made it unclear whether the idea was the author's or an idea from the previously cited source. Four versions of the passage were created in order to see the effect having a substantive title for the passage and a paragraph break between the cited argument and the argument with the ambiguous source would have on reader's perceptions of who that argument was attributable to. The results showed that the substantive title and the break in the paragraph were cues the readers took to break the attribution connection between the cited argument and the argument with the ambiguous source, which allowed more readers to believe that the source for the ambiguous argument was the writer and not the source of the first cited argument.

In a follow-up study, 60 test subjects were specifically asked to indicate any editing changes they would make to two separate versions of the same passage—one that included paragraph breaks between the cited and ambiguously sourced argument and one that did not. Only three of the respondents indicated that they would make citation changes to clarify the reference in the passage without the paragraph break and only one respondent indicated that a citation change was in order to clarify the reference in the passage with the paragraph break. The researcher interpreted this data to demonstrate that readers do not need formal citation if readers can tell the source of a piece of information either from textual clues or their own common sense.

The researcher postulated that when writers fail to make the source of a point clear through a citation, it may not be caused by a lack of knowledge of citation rules or the writer's desire to pass someone else's work off as the writer's own, but instead may be because of the perceived risk of the writer that the source will be miscommunicated to a reader. If the writer thinks the textual clues will implicitly identify the source, the choice not to cite may be due to the fact that the writer does not perceive a risk that a miscommunication will occur.

---

1. Howard Williams, Implicit Attribution, 42 Journal of Pragmatics, 617–636 (2010).

The Columbia University study may help to explain the inconsistencies new legal writers may see between the theory that all ideas taken from another source should be cited and times when that doesn't occur, like when judges issue opinions that were largely written by law clerks without attributing to those law clerks. Experienced legal readers know that judges retain law clerks specifically for the purpose of researching and writing, so the risk that a reader will think that a legal opinion was solely written by a judge is very low if there even exists a risk at all. If writers are urged to cite only when the writer perceives a risk of a miscommunication about the source of an idea, judges should feel no urge to attribute portions of their opinions written by law clerks to those law clerks.

Although the Columbia University study offers an explanation for the inconsistency of citation among various legal documents, the amount of citations in an average legal pleading may seem counter-intuitive to the Columbia University study. A student new to the law may wonder why there is a need to include a citation after every sentence in a paragraph describing a case if it is clear from the context in the sentence that the writer is describing a previously cited precedent case. The frequency of legal citation cannot be attributable to any explicit rules. Legal writing textbooks largely defer to the existing style manuals for guidance on frequency of citation. In fact, none of the legal writing textbooks reviewed for this book devotes much more than a passing reference to the frequency of citation in legal writing. It is difficult to find much guidance written down on exactly when a legal writer should cite, other than ALWD rule 34.2.

The legal writing textbooks that do mention citation frequency, indicate that the reason for citation in legal documents is twofold—first, it is a way of ensuring that the writer is being intellectually honest with the reader and not claiming ideas of others as his or her own, and second, citation demonstrates to a legal reader that there is precedent support for the claims being made in a legal document. It is this latter reason that differentiates the use of citation in legal writing from the use of citation in other genres of writing. Because the precedential nature of law is driven by a desire to minimize future conflicts by giving parties in conflict an idea of how a court will likely resolve that conflict, there is an incentive to show that analysis is built on the thoughts of others that may not be inherent in other areas of writing.

For instance, many academic disciplines reward individual, creative thoughts of a writer more highly than thoughts that are built on the ideas of others, which creates an inverse incentive for citation. But the precedential nature of law has an inherent incentive for a high amount of citation. In theory, the more citation, the more precedent supports the claims a legal writer is making. This makes the frequency of citation in legal documents squarely in line with the central outcome of the Columbia University study—an author's choice to cite is largely a calculation of risk of miscommunication. If the use of citation shows precedential support for arguments and analysis, anything short of an explicit citation runs the risk of sending the message that the analysis is not well supported and this risk is simply too high for lawyers and those studying to become lawyers.

Although frequency of citation seems to indicate that a legal analysis is well-supported, the quality of the source appears to be important for legal documents as well. In a study that analyzed the opinions of the Supreme Court, a group of political science and business professors found that the opinions of the court that cited more often to precedential cases that were frequently cited for particular propositions meant that the opinion would then be more frequently cited by later courts and would, therefore, have more precedential value.[2] Analogizing law to a web, the more frequently a case is cited for a proposition, the more "central" to the web of case law the case becomes. And subsequent cases become more "central" as well by citing to "central" cases to be pulled closer to the center of the web of law.

Legal writing is a competitive event in many contexts. Law students want to write better research and writing assignments than other law students, lawyers want to write better briefs than their opposing counsel, and judges want to write opinions that are stronger precedent for a proposition than contrary opinions written by other judges. The empirical research indicates that the frequency of citation to "centralized" cases can give a legal document a competitive edge over competing legal documents. These studies, therefore, not only highlight the importance of citation but also research. Thorough research ensures that a writer has found the most "centralized" authorities on a legal issue, which in turn, will allow the legal writer to create a more "centralized" legal document.

Citation Exercise

Which passage do you find more believable and why?

Passage 1:

The detention is unreasonable in length if the merchant fails to comply with standard procedures after he or she has recovered the goods. *Silvia v. Zayre Corporation*, 233 So. 2d 856, 858 (Fla. 3d Dist. App. 1970). In *Silvia*, the store's

---

2. Frank B. Cross, et. al., Citations in the U.S. Supreme Court: An Empirical study of their Use and Significance, 2010 Univ. of Ill. L.R. 489 (2010).

security officers apprehended the customer for shoplifting and took him to the detention room. *Id.* at 858 n.1. After other store employees recovered the merchandise, the officers coerced and interrogated the customer for over three hours before turning him over to the police. *Id.* The court said this was an unreasonable amount of time because there was a large time gap after the goods were recovered before the police arrived.

Passage 2:

Florida courts find a detention is unreasonable in length if the merchant fails to comply with standard procedures after he or she has recovered the goods. Standard procedures should be set up so that a person is released after the store recovers the merchandise.

PART IV

Concepts for Writing Persuasive Documents

Chapter 15

How Do You Persuade in Legal Writing?

This question is arguably the most important question asked in this book. It is also the most controversial as far as the research is concerned. An incredible amount of research and science has focused on what persuades. Unfortunately, very little of it addresses legal writing. Most advice given about persuasion as it relates to legal writing is still at the theoretical stage, and the empirical evidence that exists seems to be somewhat inconsistent.

The question of what persuades is not limited to memoranda submitted to a court or to an opposing party. All legal writing is persuasive to some degree. Most legal writing texts distinguish between "objective writing" and "persuasive writing."[1] In fact, some legal writing texts only address "objective" writing,[2] and others address only "persuasive" writing.[3] In many law schools, legal writing classes are divided into Legal Research and Writing I, which teaches objective writing, and Legal Research and Writing II, which teaches persuasive writing.

The problem with such a distinction is that it obscures the fact that all legal writing has some level of persuasion to it. Even "objective" writing, such as an inter-office memorandum, or a client letter, is persuasive writing in the sense that the writer is trying to convince the reader that the writer is correct. In an office memorandum, the writer is trying to convince the reader that the analysis is fair and balanced and presents, in a thorough, yet efficient, manner, an accurate assessment of the law as it relates to a client's issue. In that sense, the

---

1. *See e.g.* Richard K. Neumann, Jr., *Legal Reasoning and Legal Writing* (Aspen 5th ed. 2005), which addresses objective writing and then "shifts" to persuasive writing, and John C. Dernbach et al., *Legal Writing & Legal Method* (Aspen 4th ed. 2010).

2. The Coughlin text, *A Lawyer Writes,* is an example of a textbook that addresses only "objective" writing.

3. For example Michael Smith's *Advanced Legal Writing* is aimed at "persuasive" writing.

writer is trying to persuade the reader that the writer "got it right," although this persuasion may not be as "one-sided" as persuasion made to a court.

The same is true of memoranda submitted to the court and to an opposing party. The writer is trying to convince the reader that the writer "got it right." So, is there a difference between "persuasion" in objective writing and "persuasion" in persuasive writing? Even if so, what are the elements that make legal writing persuasive in either case?

Legal writing texts are full of advice for rendering a "persuasive" document more persuasive. Most of the advice is pragmatic and reflects what is usually considered good practice in the legal world, but little of it is explicitly backed by scientific studies or statistical analyses. When the reason for the advice does not seem readily apparent, it might be helpful to back up the reasoning with some science. But some advice is readily seen to be likely to persuade.

For example, Richard Neumann states that it is persuasive to use simple and concrete words that will paint a picture in a reader's mind. He provides this example:

> This is not simple and concrete:

> Where contamination has occurred, lead dust can be ingested by young children through frequent and unpredictable hand-mouth contact during play.

> This is:

> If the floor inside a building or the soil outside is contaminated with lead dust, young children can literally eat lead because they frequently and unexpectedly put their hands and other things in their mouths while playing.[4]

Even though there is no scientific explanation as to why the second sentence is more powerful than the first, it is probably not needed.

While most legal writing texts do not claim a scientific basis for why a particular practice is more persuasive, there are some that do. One in particular, *Advanced Legal Writing: Theories and Strategies in Persuasive Writing*, written by Michael R. Smith, provides not only advice on persuasion, but also provides some bases for the advice proffered.[5] Smith bases his book on the classi-

---

4. Neumann, *Legal Reasoning and Legal Writing*, 329.

5. Michael R. Smith, *Advanced Legal Writing: Theories and Strategies in Persuasive Writing* (Aspen 3rd ed. 2013). A conference based on Smith's book "A Dialogue About Persuasion in Legal Writing & Lawyering" held on September 19, 2008 at Rutgers School of Law— Camden. A summary of the conference can be found at Legal Writing Prof Blog: http://

cal rhetorical devices of logos, pathos, and ethos as the basis for effective persuasion.[6] For logos, which is the traditional, logical, rule-based reasoning used by lawyers (the deductive reasoning and CREAC structure treated in chapters 5 and 11), Smith accepts the structure as valid without resort to research or support, but then uses cognitive psychology theory to show that legal rules should be supplemented with illustrative narratives in order to make the CREAC persuasive:

> A short answer to the question of why narrative has such communicative power is that a person learns through story in the same way that he or she learns through experience. Starting at infancy, human beings learn by interacting with and experiencing the world around them. And because life is continual and occurs over the passage of time, much of learning by experience happens as events, ideas, and concepts build on each other. A person is basically the protagonist in the story that is his or her own life. And much of what we learn is learned by chronologically experiencing related events that build on each other.[7]

Although Smith does not discuss the studies underpinning his claim that narrative makes rule-based reasoning more persuasive, he cites sources that discuss some of those studies.[8] Similar psychological studies supporting the idea that narrative is a superior vehicle for conveying information are set forth in Chapter 10.

Next, Smith tackles pathos as an effective device for persuasion. Pathos is an appeal to the reader's emotions, which is also an appeal to the reader's values, which underlie those emotions.[9] Smith relies on Neumann's explanation of motivating (pathos) arguments and justifying (logos) arguments[10] to set forth his thesis that the stronger the logos argument, the less need there is for a pathos argument and the weaker the logos, the more need for pathos.[11] Smith's explanation of the theory underlying the persuasiveness of pathos arguments is excellent, but it does not reference any empirical evidence underlying the theory.

---

lawprofessors.typepad.com/legalwriting/2008/09/page/2/. The conference centered around whether logos or pathos was the most persuasive basis for making a legal argument. There was no clear winner.

6. *Id.* at 11–13.

7. *Id.* at 38–39.

8. *Id.*

9. *Id.* at 91.

10. *Id.* at 104–05.

11. *Id.* at 105.

Finally, Smith adds in the element of ethos. For Smith, ethos is primarily evincing credibility and intelligence on the part of the advocate (for our purposes, the writer), and he believes this may be the most important form of persuasion:

> A strong argument can be made that ethos is more important to persuasive legal writing than either logical argument (logos) or appeals to emotion (pathos). In fact, the effectiveness of both emotional and logical arguments depends in large part on perceptions of the advocate's credibility. Consider, for example, the role of credibility in an emotional appeal. A highly emotional argument, if presented by someone with little credibility, will likely be met with skepticism rather than acceptance.[12]

Again, the explanation and application of the theory of ethos is thorough and on point, but is not expressly supported by any empirical evidence. As practitioners and legal writing professors we can wholly endorse Smith's use of classical rhetoric as applied to legal writing, but is it supported by science or other empirical evidence?

The answer is probably yes. The effectiveness of using logos, pathos, and ethos to persuade is supported by the general literature of persuasion and to the extent such studies exist, by legal writing research.

Logos

As mentioned above in Chapter 5, syllogistic reasoning is supported by its similarity to the mathematical property of transitivity. The legal writing formulation of syllogistic reasoning, CREAC, has been shown by analogy to related studies to be more effective because it places important information first, it is organized rather than disorganized, and it is a familiar format for the reader.

Further empirical support for the superior persuasiveness of a logos-based argument can be found in the "priming" studies that have been applied to CREAC-type organization by Kathryn Stanchi to suggest that the most important, and most emotionally potent, information should be put early in a memo, ideally in a heading or an early paragraph, to prime the thinking of the reader to be sympathetic to the writer's argument.[13] Of course, as discussed in Chap-

---

12. *Id.* at 125.

13. Kathryn M. Stanchi, *The Power of Priming in Legal Advocacy: Using the Science of First Impressions to Persuade the Reader*, 89 Or. L. Rev. 305 (2010–2011).

ter 2, the validity of many of the priming studies have been questioned by subsequent studies that were unable to replicate the results of the initial studies.

Additional support for the CREAC articulation of logos reasoning can be gleaned from surveys of judges. Judges seem to like "tried and true" organizational schemes. In one such survey of 355 federal court judges (representing 46% of the sitting judges at the time), the "judges seem[ed] to prefer "tried and true" organizational forms, including summaries of or roadmaps to arguments and the selection of fewer strong arguments arranged in their order of importance."[14] In the same study, the majority of judges said that the organization of the argument was second only to the analysis.[15] It's probably fair to say that logos and CREAC persuade.

Pathos

Apart from the use of narrative in making an argument based on pathos, as explained in Chapter 10, there is little empirical evidence in the legal writing literature showing that appeals to emotions or values are persuasive. However, recent neuroscience research using brain functional magnetic resonance imaging suggests that emotions and feelings play a vital role in all decision making processes, and that the areas of the brain responsible for emotions are accessed before areas of the brain that are responsible for rational and conscious thought. In other words, we make our decisions based on emotion and unconscious mental processes, and a rational argument is simply a mechanism the brain uses to justify its previous decision based on emotion.[16]

---

14. Kristen K. Robbins, The Inside Scoop: What Federal Judges Really Think About the Way Lawyers Write 8 Legal Writing: J. Legal Writing Inst. 284 (2002).

15. *Id.* at 271.

16. *See e.g.* Antoine Bechara, Hanna Damasio, and Antonio Damasio, Emotion, Decision Making and the Orbitofrontal Cortex, Cereb. Cortex (2000) 10 (3): 295–307 (reviewing studies showing that "decision making is a process that is influenced by marker signals that arise in bioregulatory processes, including those that express themselves in emotions and feelings."); Chun Siong Soon, Marcel Brass, Hans-Jochen Heinze, & John-Dylan Haynes, Unconscious Determinants of Free Decisions in the Human Brain, 11 Nature Neuroscience 5, 543 (May 2008) ("[T]he outcome of a decision can be encoded in brain activity of prefrontal and parietal cortex up to 10 [seconds] before it enters awareness. This delay presumably reflects the operation of a network of high-level control areas that begin to prepare an upcoming decision long before it enters awareness."); Marina Krakovsky, *How Do We Decide?*, http://www.gsb.stanford.edu/news/bmag/sbsm0802/feature-babashiv.html (an interview with Professor Baba Shiv, which reviews the seminal works of Daniel Kahneman, Amos Tversky and Antonion Damasio on the role of emotion in decision making); Evan R.

The researchers used functional magnetic resonance imaging (fMRI) to map the areas of the brain where there was an increase in the flow of blood. The theory is that increased blood flow equates to increased neural activity. While undergoing the non-invasive fMRI, the researchers performed the following experiment:

> The subjects were asked to relax while fixating on the center of the screen where a stream of letters was presented. At some point, when they felt the urge to do so, they were to freely decide between one of two buttons, operated by the left and right index fingers, and press it immediately. In parallel, they should remember the letter presented when their motor decision was consciously made. After subjects pressed their freely chosen response button, a 'response mapping' screen with four choices appeared. The subjects indicated when they had made their motor decision by selecting the corresponding letter with a second button press.[17]

The scientists found that they were able to predict which button the subjects were going to push *up to ten seconds before the subjects consciously decided which button to push* by analyzing the blood flow to the unconscious areas of the brain—areas which also govern emotion.[18]

Other scientists have found that subjects who have experienced trauma, tumors, or other damage to areas of the brain that control emotion struggled to make decisions more than those without such damage.[19] While such research does not directly implicate legal writing, it may suggest that arguments based on emotion or pathos may affect decision making more than we previously suspected.

Research cited by Kathryn Stanchi suggests that a judge's decision-making can be affected by properly understanding which areas of brain processing are affected by various arguments and should be considered before using an argument intended to elicit an emotional response.[20] Her argument is complex, however, and would be difficult for some legal writers to implement.

Goldstein, *The Anatomy of Influence*, The Chronicle of Higher Education, https://chronicle.com/article/The-Anatomy-of-Influence/129688/ (same).

17. Chun Siong Soon, Marcel Brass, Hans-Jochen Heinze, & John-Dylan Haynes, 543.

18. *Id.*

19. Antoine Bechara, Hanna Damasio, and Antonio Damasio, *Emotion, Decision Making and the Orbitofrontal Cortex*, Cereb. Cortex (2000) 10 (3): 295–307.

20. Kathryn M. Stanchi, *The Science of Persuasion: An Initial Exploration*, 2006 MICH. ST. L. REV. 1, 25–38.

Ethos

There is some research indicating that ethos (the credibility of a lawyer), like pathos, affects the persuasiveness of a legal argument. Generally, most scholars and psychologists agree that establishing credibility is an important aspect of legal persuasion. The expertise and trustworthiness of a lawyer,[21] good legal writing, which includes readability and a lack of technical errors in legal writing submitted to a court,[22] and the appropriate disclosure of adverse facts and law all add to a lawyer's credibility.[23]

While no research shows the relative importance of logos, pathos, or ethos, it is safe to say that the most recent research in neuroscience, psychology, and all behavioral sciences suggests that a legal writer should consider all three bases for persuasion in the writer's arguments to a court. Now, if scientists can just tell us how to fit all of that persuasion into fifteen pages of a brief, we would never lose a case!

---

21. Melissa Weresh does the best job of using the available science to make this point in *Morality, Trust, and Illusion: Ethos as Relationship*, 9 Legal Commun. & Rhetoric: JALWD 229 (2012).

22. *See* Long & Christensen, *Clearly, Using Intensifiers*, *supra* note 8, at 176; Charles A. Bird & Webster Burke Kinnaird, *Objective Analysis of Advocacy Preferences and Prevalent Mythologies in One California Appellate Court*, 4 J. App. Prac. & Process 141, 153 (2002); David Lewis, *If You Have Seen One Circuit, Have You Seen Them All? A Comparison of the Advocacy Preferences of Three Federal Circuit Courts of Appeal*, 8 Denv. U. L. Rev. 893, 908 (2006); *see also* David Lewis, *What's the Difference? Comparing the Advocacy Preferences of State and Federal Appellate Judges*, 7 J. App. Prac. & Process 335, 350 (2005).

23. Jennifer K. Robbenold & Jean R. Sternlight, *Psychology for Lawyers*, 360–61 and accompanying footnotes (2012).

Chapter 16

Do Intensifiers Really Intensify?[*]

For somewhat inexplicable reasons, law students and lawyers love to emphasize the strength of an argument by adding an intensifier to a sentence, despite the fact that scholars have generally found that overusing intensifiers (words such as "clearly," "obviously," and "very") negatively affects the persuasiveness or credibility of a legal argument. Even if a claimed proposition is not at all "clear," lawyers seem almost compelled to claim that "clearly" their proposition is correct.

Until recently, no one had studied whether using a lot of intensifiers in legal documents affected the efficacy of those documents. Professors Long and Christensen, however, examined actual appellate briefs to determine whether a relationship exists between intensifier use and the outcome of an appeal. Their empirical study of appellate briefs has shown that the frequent use of intensifiers in appellate briefs (particularly by an appellant) is usually associated with a statistically significant increase in adverse outcomes for an "offending" party. But—and this was a somewhat unusual result—if an appellate opinion uses a high rate of intensifiers, an appellant's brief written for that appeal that also uses a high rate of intensifiers is associated with a statistically significant increase in favorable outcomes.

Their study further found that when a dissenting opinion is written, judges use significantly more intensifiers in both the majority and dissenting opinions. In other words, as things become less clear, judges tend to use "clearly" and "obviously" more often. This result can be interpreted several ways. It may be that overusing intensifiers actually renders a brief suspect and subject to increased skepticism by appellate court judges. Alternatively, it may be that the overuse of intensifiers is accompanied by violations of other writing conventions that further affect the credibility of the brief. Or, it may simply be that appellants or appellees with difficult arguments (arguments they believe they are likely to lose) tend to lapse into an intensifier-rich mode of writing in an attempt to bolster the perceived weaknesses of an argument. All of these fac-

---

[*] This chapter is adapted from Lance N. Long and William F. Christensen, *Clearly, Using Intensifiers Is Very Bad, Or Is It?* 45 Idaho Law Review 171 (Fall 2008).

tors may combine to produce the result. Of course, since no causal relationship is shown, it could be a yet unidentified factor.

The problem of lawyers claiming that their client "clearly" is in the right has been addressed by many jurists, including the Chief Justice of the Supreme Court. Addressing students and faculty at Northwestern University School of Law, Chief Justice John Roberts commented on the use of intensifiers in legal briefs:

> We get hundreds and hundreds of briefs, and they're all the same.... Somebody says, "My client clearly deserves to win, the cases clearly do this, the language clearly reads this," blah, blah blah. And you pick up the other side and, lo and behold, they think they clearly deserve to win.
>
> How about a little recognition that it's a tough job?
>
> ...
>
> I mean, if it was an easy case, we wouldn't have it.[1]

Perhaps unknowingly, the Chief Justice ratified the nearly universal advice of legal writing scholars and experts, who unequivocally recommend avoiding intensifiers such as "obviously" and "clearly."[2] Richard Neumann explained the reasoning for this admonition: "Judges assume that expressions like these are used to cover up a lack of logical proof."[3]

---

1. Robert Barnes, *Chief Justice Counsels Humility: Roberts Says Lawyers Must Put Themselves in Judges' Shoes*, WASH. POST, Feb. 6, 2007, at A15.

2. *See, e.g.*, MARY BETH BEAZLEY, A PRACTICAL GUIDE TO APPELLATE ADVOCACY 194 (2d ed. 2006) ("*Clearly, obviously, of course,* and *it is evident that* have been so overused that they go beyond having no meaning to having a negative meaning."); BRADLEY G. CLARY & PAMELA LYSAGHT, SUCCESSFUL LEGAL ANALYSIS AND WRITING: THE FUNDAMENTALS 102 (2d ed. 2006) ("Let nouns and verbs do most of your talking, not adjectives and adverbs. Particularly avoid exaggeration through conclusory modifiers such as 'clearly,' 'plainly,' 'very,' 'obviously,' 'outrageous,' 'unconscionable,' and the like."); LINDA H. EDWARDS, LEGAL WRITING AND ANALYSIS 277 (2003) ("Because generations of writers have overused words like 'clearly' or 'very,' these and other common intensifiers have become virtually meaningless. As a matter of fact, they have begun to develop a connotation exactly opposite their original meaning."); BRYAN A. GARNER, THE REDBOOK: A MANUAL ON LEGAL STYLE 224 (2d ed. 2006) ("[C]learly; obviously. As sentence adverbs <Clearly, this is true>, these weasel words are often exaggerators. They may reassure the writer but not the reader. If something is clearly or obviously true, then prove it to the reader without resorting to the conclusory use of these words."); RICHARD K. NEUMANN, JR., LEGAL REASONING AND LEGAL WRITING: STRUCTURE, STRATEGY, AND STYLE 330 (5th ed. 2005) ("'It is obvious' and 'clearly' supply no extra meaning. Instead, they divert the reader's attention from the message of the sentence.").

3. NEUMANN *supra* n. 3 at 330.

Although Chief Justice Roberts is not fond of using the word "clearly," and although legal writing texts consider intensifier use in legal briefs inappropriate and maybe even harmful, is there any empirical evidence that using intensifiers could actually negatively affect the outcome of an appeal? Scholarly studies of intensifier use in other legal and non-legal settings suggest, subject to some exceptions, that intensifier use may negatively affect the perception of the subject matter containing intensifiers or the person using intensifiers.

The problem addressed by the Long and Christensen study is easily identified in almost any legal document. For example, a random selection of two or three appellate briefs from an online database demonstrates the prolific use of intensifiers. Long and Christensen did exactly that, and in the first brief randomly selected, the intensifiers "very" and "certainly" were used six times in twelve pages. In the second brief, the intensifiers "very," "clearly," "patently," "absolutely," "undoubtedly," "certainly," and "simply" were used forty-seven times in a fifty-nine-page brief.

Noting the pervasive use of intensifiers, authors of legal writing texts, style manuals, and practitioner guides have universally attacked their use,[4] claiming that intensifiers are "virtually meaningless"[5] or even harmful because they have been historically overused; "they go beyond having no meaning to having a negative meaning."[6] Legal writing expert Bryan Garner notes that the terms "clearly" and "obviously" "may reassure the writer but not the reader. If something is clearly or obviously true, prove it to the reader without resorting to the conclusory use of these words."[7] Richard Wydick eloquently summarizes the same idea: "If what is said is clear, then 'clearly' is not needed, and if it is

---

4. *See e.g.* ROBERTO ARON ET AL., TRIAL COMMUNICATION SKILLS §15.06 (2d ed. 2007) ("The *powerless* style is characterized by the frequent use of such linguistic features as intensifiers...."); DAVID M. BRODSKY, BUSINESS AND COMMERCIAL LITIGATION IN FEDERAL COURTS §34:15 (Robert L. Haig ed., 2d ed. 2005) ("Counsel should eliminate all forms of powerless speech in opening statements ... [including] intensifiers, such as 'very' or 'definitely'...."); TED A. DONNER & RICHARD K. GABRIEL, JURY SELECTION STRATEGY AND SCIENCE §21:4 (3d ed. 2007) ("Powerless speech is characterized by more frequent use of intensifiers (e.g. 'so,' 'very,' or 'too,' as in 'I like him SO much')....").

5. EDWARDS *supra* n. 3 at 277; *see also* RAY & RAMSFIELD at 204 ("Also avoid modifiers that have little substantive meaning, such as ... 'very,' or 'obviously.'") (quotation marks added); DuVivier at 1511 ("[A]dding an intensifier may be superfluous.").

6. BEAZLEY *supra* n. 3 at 194; *see also* NEUMANN *supra* n. 3 at 330 ("You can do harm with words that claim too much."); Stein, *supra* note 7, at 46 ("[Intensifiers] make you sound uncertain.").

7. GARNER *supra* n. 2 at 224.

not clear, then 'clearly' will not make it so."[8] The universal theme is that intensifiers, at best, create unnecessary clutter or, at worst, through chronic overuse, negate their intended purpose by causing a reader to question, rather than be reassured by, the proposition being intensified.

Legal writing authorities and practitioners are not the only groups suggesting that the excessive use of intensifiers may negatively affect participants in legal proceedings. Judges also seem to be annoyed and concerned by intensifier use. In addition to Chief Justice Roberts's excoriation of inappropriately using the word "clearly,"[9] surveys of justices and judges have indicated a similar disapproval of intensifier use.

In a 2001 survey of San Diego, California-based appellate court judges and staff attorneys, conducted by Charles A. Bird and Webster Burke Kinnaird, the respondents generally reported that they were bothered by the "use of adverbs such as 'clearly' and 'obviously' in place of logic or authority...."[10] In a series of later surveys conducted by David Lewis, all based on the California survey, both federal and state appellate judges were asked whether "[i]t bothers [them] when a brief uses adverbs like 'clearly' and 'obviously' to support arguments."[11] All the studies reported similar results: judges mildly to somewhat strongly agreed that such use of adverbs bothered them.[12]

An informal survey of federal judges and clerks in the District of Utah showed similar results. Judges and clerks were asked which of the following two sentences they thought was more persuasive: "It is obvious, therefore, that the defendant clearly understood the consequences of his acts," and "[t]herefore, the defendant understood the consequences of his acts."[13] Fifteen out of the nineteen respondents answered that the second sentence was "more persuasive" than the first, one answered that the second was "slightly more persuasive" than the first, two answered that both sentences were "equally persuasive," and one answered that the first sentence was "slightly more persuasive." Twelve of the respondents also answered that they would tend to view

---

8. DuVivier *supra* n. 4 at 1511 (quotation marks added) (quoting RICHARD C. WYDICK, PLAIN ENGLISH FOR LAWYERS 67 (2d ed. 1985)).

9. *See* Barnes *supra* n. 1 at A15.

10. Charles A. Bird & Webster Burke Kinnaird, *Objective Analysis of Advocacy Preferences and Prevalent Mythologies in One California Appellate Court*, 4 J. APP. PRAC. & PROCESS 141, 153 (2002).

11. David Lewis, *If You Have Seen One Circuit, Have You Seen Them All? A Comparison of the Advocacy Preferences of Three Federal Circuit Courts of Appeal*, 8 DENV. U. L. REV. 893, 908 (2006).

12. Lewis, *Comparison*.

13. NEUMANN *supra* n. 3 at 330.

a brief that used the first sentence as "less credible," while seven respondents answered that neither sentence would affect their assessment of the brief's credibility.

Judicial scorn for using intensifiers is also reflected in the restyling of the Federal Rules of Civil Procedure, which minimizes the use of redundant intensifiers.[14] On the other hand, as discussed below, despite the apparent disdain for intensifiers, judges seem to use intensifiers in judicial opinions almost as much as, and in some cases much more than, practitioners.

Apart from legal scholars, lawyers, and judges, the effect of using intensifiers in both legal and non-legal communication has also been the subject of scholarly examination and numerous empirical studies in various disciplines over the last fifty years.[15] Not all of these studies support the conclusions and opinions of legal writing authorities, practitioners, and judges. As early as 1959, a study showed that intensifiers do, in fact, intensify—at least if the reaction of a listener or reader to the same sentence first without and then, immediately thereafter, with the intensifier is considered.[16] In that study, "the intensifier 'very' was shown to have a scalar value of approximately 1.25."[17] Put another way, if the word "good" has a "favorability value" of 1.16, then "'very good' carries a favorability factor of approximately 1.45 (1.16 x 1.25)."[18] Other studies have corroborated this finding.[19]

However, a study of social survey questions found that, if not paired with a question omitting the intensifier, the effect of adding an intensifier to a survey question was insignificant.[20] For example, there was little difference in responses

---

14. Lee H. Rosenthal, THE RESTYLED FEDERAL RULES OF CIVIL PROCEDURE, (A.L.I.-A.B.A. Course of Study March 7–9, 2007) WL SM090 1; *see also* Joseph Kimble, *Guiding Principles for Restyling the Federal Rules of Civil Procedure (Part 2)*, 84 MICH. B.J. 52, 52 (2005); Charles Delafuente, *Refining Legal Language*, 4 A.B.A. J. E-REP. 3 (2005).

15. *See* Norman Cliff, *Adverbs as Multipliers*, 66 PSYCHOL. REV. 27 (1959); John M. Conley et al., *The Power of Language: Presentational Style in the Courtroom*, 1978 DUKE L.J. 1375 (1978); Bonnie Erickson et al., *Speech Style and Impression Formation in a Court Setting: The Effects of "Powerful" and "Powerless" Speech*, 14 J. EXPERIMENTAL & SOC. PSYCHOL. 266 (1978); Colm A. O'Muircheartaigh et al., *Intensifiers in Behavioral Frequency Questions*, 57 PUB. OPINION Q. 552 (1993).

16. Cliff *supra* n. 14 at 30.

17. O'Muircheartaigh et al. *supra* n. 18 at 553.

18. *Id.*; *see also* Edward E. Smith et al., *Combining Prototypes: A Selective Modification Model*, 12 COGNITIVE SCI. 485 (1988) (finding similar results to the Cliff study using the words "very" and "slightly").

19. *See* O'Muircheartaigh et al. *supra* n. 18 (finding that a survey question asked first without and then with an intensifier produced a response shift); Smith et al. (finding similar results using the words "very" and "slightly" paired to the color of fruits).

20. O'Muircheartaigh et al. *supra* n. 18 at 552.

by subjects who were asked whether they were "really annoyed" by a television commercial and those who were asked whether they were "annoyed" by a television commercial.[21] This result supports the claim of legal writing professionals and practitioners that intensifiers are meaningless or superfluous.[22]

But are intensifiers actually harmful, as suggested by Neumann and Beazley?[23] In 1975, Robin Lakoff raised that question in her groundbreaking book, *Language and Woman's Place*.[24] Lakoff suggested that using "intensives" (particularly the word "so") was one aspect of women's speech that reflected a woman's lesser "real-world power compared with a man."[25] Therefore, according to Lakoff, the use of intensifiers can be a negative indicator and perpetuator of lesser power in the real world.

Taking their cue in part from Lakoff, William O'Barr and others proposed that using intensifiers was one of several forms of "powerless language" and, when used by witnesses in a courtroom, "strongly affects how favorably a witness is perceived and by implication suggests that these sorts of differences may play a consequential role in the legal process itself."[26] Powerless language includes using hedges, (such as "sort of," "kind of," "a little"), hesitations (such as "ah," "um," "let's see"), answering a question with rising intonation ("thirty-five?"), polite forms, ("please," "thank you") and other language forms originally associated by Lakoff with female speech.[27]

In two studies performed by O'Barr and others, the frequent use of intensifiers, as part of powerless language, was shown to have a significant correlation with lower ratings of witness veracity, competence, and intelligence.[28] These studies are significant for legal writing professionals and practitioners because they specifically apply the concept of powerless language to a legal con-

---

21. *Id.* at 552–53. One interesting exception was that the phrase "extreme physical pain" produced a pronounced response shift in comparison to the phrase "physical pain." *Id.*

22. *See* EDWARDS *supra* n. 3 at 194; DuVivier, at 1511.

23. BEAZLEY *supra* n. 3 at 277; NEUMANN at 330.

24. ROBIN TOLMACH LAKOFF, LANGUAGE AND WOMAN'S PLACE 3 (Mary Bucholtz ed., 2004).

25. *Id.* at 82.

26. WILLIAM M. O'BARR, LINGUISTIC EVIDENCE: LANGUAGE, POWER, AND STRATEGY IN THE COURTROOM 75 (Donald Black ed., 1982).

27. *Id.* at 63–75. Interestingly, later studies have found that many forms of powerless speech are not necessarily related to female speech. *See* CONLEY & O'BARR, *supra* note 29, at 64–66; James J. Bradac & Anthony Mulac, *Men's and Women's Use of Intensifiers and Hedges in Problem-Solving Interaction: Molar and Molecular Analyses*, 28 RES. ON LANGUAGE & SOC. INTERACTION 93, 109–11 (1995).

28. O'BARR *supra* n. 25 at 74; JOHN M. CONLEY WILLIAM O'BARR, JUST WORDS 64 (2d ed. 2005).

text and show that the use of powerless language is not necessarily a gender-based phenomenon, but instead extends to any witness that speaks "a language of deference, subordination, and nonassertiveness...."[29] Furthermore, the effect was found in both oral and written language.[30]

Later studies by Lawrence Hosman and others have further explored the findings of O'Barr and his colleagues and have focused on particular forms of powerful and powerless speech, including the use of intensifiers.[31] Although some of these studies seem to corroborate the conclusion that intensifiers, as a form of powerless speech, will likely generate less favorable perceptions of competence and credibility,[32] other studies have found that intensifiers, when isolated from other recognized forms of powerless speech, actually become powerful speech.[33]

In a recent study simulating defendant testimony in a criminal trial, Hosman and Siltanen isolated the effect of intensifiers from the effects of other types of powerless speech, in particular, hedges and hesitations—and found that intensifiers were "evaluated positively" by the recipients.[34] He concluded that "intensifiers should not be considered a powerless form of language," and noted that this conclusion "confirms other studies ... that have found that intensifiers are perceived as powerful forms...."[35] Nonetheless, The study's authors caution against reading too much into this conclusion, noting "several studies have failed to find that intensifiers had a significant independent impact in the presence of other language variables such as hedges and hesitations."[36]

Despite extensive scholarly treatment, it remains unclear whether using intensifiers in legal writing is harmful. Currently, the best characterization of

---

29. CONLEY & O'BARR *supra* n. 29 at 65. *Just Words* is a must read for anyone wanting an overview of the past thirty years of law and language research and the current trends in that field.

30. Erickson et al. *supra* n. 14 at 269–78.

31. *See, e.g.*, Lawrence A. Hosman, *The Evaluative Consequences of Hedges, Hesitations, and Intensifiers*, 15 HUM. COMM. RES. 383, 384–85, 401 (1989); Lawrence A. Hosman & Susan A. Siltanen, *Powerful and Powerless Language Forms: Their Consequences for Impression Formation, Attributions of Control of Self and Control of Others, Cognitive Responses, and Message Memory*, 25 J. LANGUAGE & SOC. PSYCHOL. 33, 43–44 (2006); Calvin Morrill & Peter C. Facciola, *The Power of Language in Adjudication and Mediation: Institutional Contexts as Predictors of Social Evaluation*, 17 LAW & SOC. INQUIRY 191, 208, 212 (1992).

32. Hosman *supra* n. 30 at 384–85, 401; Bradac & Mulac, *Powerful and Powerless Speech* at 339; Morrill & Facciola *supra* n. 30 at 208.

33. Hosman & Siltanen; Hosman; Bradac & Mulac, *Men's and Women's*; Bradac & Mulac, *Powerful and Powerless Speech*.

34. Hosman & Siltanen *supra* n. 30 at 43.

35. *Id.*

36. *Id.* at 44.

the literature seems to suggest that intensifiers, if isolated from other forms of powerless speech, or if used in simultaneous comparison with a phrase omitting the intensifier, actually do what intensifiers were originally meant to do—they intensify. On the other hand, when used in connection with other forms of powerless speech and without reference to a phrase lacking the given intensifier, they may negatively affect the writer or speaker's perceived credibility or competence—they "detensify."

Interestingly, even though some later studies have found that intensifiers, when isolated from other forms of powerless speech, are positively evaluated, most practitioner materials have apparently not caught up with the more recent research and continue to suggest that using intensifiers is always improper, always harmful, or always associated with powerless speech.[37]

Despite the extensive treatment of intensifiers in scholarly literature, until the Long/Christensen study no research had specifically addressed the question of whether the use of intensifiers will be perceived negatively in appellate briefs. Legal writing experts and scholars have assumed that the same principles that govern the use of intensifiers in legal advocacy and writing generally will also apply to appellate briefs and have implicitly, if not explicitly, assumed that appellate judges will react to intensifiers in the same way as other audiences.[38] The question is interesting because, although the traditional wisdom and opinions of legal writing authorities, practitioners, and judges claim that intensifier use will be negatively perceived in appellate briefs, the findings of Hosman and others suggest that it might not. Appellate briefs provide a unique vehicle for studying intensifier use because appellate briefs tend to use intensifiers but do not tend to use hedges, and because they are written, they do not contain hesitations. Therefore, a study relating intensifier use in appellate briefs with the outcome of the appeal could arguably test Hosman's simulated results in

---

37. *See, e.g.*, Aron et al; Brodsky; Donner & Gabriel; Dunne; National Jury Project, Inc.; Block; Conlin; Stein.

38. *See, e.g.*, Gerald Lebovits, *Legal-Writing Myths—Part 1*, N.Y. St. B.J., Feb. 2006, at 56, 64 ("Techniques that fail with judges are … using intensifiers and qualifiers.…"); Marilyn Bush LeLeiko, *Effective Legal Writing: A Hands-On Workshop Materials* 247, 283 (PLI New York Practice Skills Course Handbook Series No. F0-300K, Feb./May 1999), WL 43 PLI/NY 247 ("Eliminate meaningless modifiers and empty intensifiers such as … very, quite, really, truly, actually, obviously") (emphasis omitted); Barbara A. Lukeman, *The Ins and Outs of the Appellate Brief* 51, 59 (NBI Appeals A to Z: From Post Trial Motions to Oral Argument 2007), WL 36992 NBI-CLE 51 ("[A]void overly confident language such as 'clearly.' By inserting words such as 'clearly' or 'obviously' you tend to raise the bar for you and your client. A judge may agree with your position, but not your assertion that it is clear or obvious.").

a real-life legal setting. It is also interesting because both Hosman and Morrill suggest that law and language research needs to be more directed towards "outcomes" (although they probably did not have "appellate outcomes" in mind).[39]

Of course, on a more practical level, judges and clerks should discern between the appropriate use of intensifiers and the overuse of intensifiers in an attempt to bolster an argument. Long and Christensen did not answer the question of whether excessive intensifier use *causes* an increased likelihood of a negative result on appeal, but it did show that the rate of intensifier use was associated with a statistically significant change in the likelihood of success on appeal.

Long and Christensen randomly selected 400 state and federal court appellate cases. Statistical regression was used to evaluate the impact of appellant and appellee intensifier rates ("IRs") on the odds of reversal. The analysis indicated that state cases have 2.46 times higher odds of reversal than federal cases (p-value < 0.0001). Cases with dissents have 1.81 times the odds of reversal as cases where there were no dissenting judges (p-value = 0.0308). The appellant IR has a complicated but significant effect on the odds of reversal, but the appellee's IR was not statistically significant (with a p-value of 0.80 when added to the model).

The study found that increased intensifier usage has a non-significant effect on appellees and a mixed effect on appellants. As the appellant's IR increases, the odds of reversal generally decreases. However, this negative impact of appellant intensifier usage is mitigated (or even reversed) as the IR in the judge's opinion increases. While none of these relationships between intensifier usage and judicial decisions are necessarily causal, there is some evidence that the effect of an appellant's intensifier usage will change with the rate of intensifiers used by the judge who writes the opinion. Although the study made no claim about the causality of intensifier use as it relates to judges' decisions, there is some reason to believe that a judge's response to intensifiers in appellant and appellee briefs may depend on the judge's own use of intensifiers.

Despite judges and legal writing scholars generally denouncing the use of intensifiers, the odds of reversal can actually be higher for appellants who have high intensifier usage rates but only when the judge writing the opinion is also a prodigious user of intensifiers. For the majority of cases, however, the conventional wisdom that intensifiers are associated with losing arguments is validated. Although it is far from clear, the Long/Christensen study suggests that intensifiers should be used with care in appellate briefs and, by extrapolation, in all legal memoranda.

---

39. Morrill & Facciola *supra* n. 30 at 212.

Chapter 17

Is Less More?

Every one of the legal writing books we surveyed has at least some portion of a chapter, if not many chapters, devoted to stylistic choices that can affect the readability and comprehensibility of a legal writer's prose, and many of these stylistic choices were offered in the sections of these books that explain the techniques of persuasive writing. These stylistic choices seem to be more art than science because they do not appear to change the substance of the writing. So when a textbook cautions a reader against using legalese, a law student may feel that changing "within said time" to "within the time" is simply the preference of textbook authors or law professors, but doesn't change a reader's ability to comprehend the student's writing. Or when a textbook indicates that simple language is clearer for the reader and, therefore, more powerful for persuasive writing, a law student may feel as if this is just a guess on the part of the author.

It turns out that many of these pieces of stylistic advice happen to have a basis in science. In the early 1990s the National Center for Educational Statistics conducted a study and discovered that the average adult in the United States reads at an 8th to 9th-grade level.[1] The same study indicated that the average person in the United States with a post-graduate degree reads at above a 10th-grade level. While the average attorney, presumably, reads at the same above-10th-grade level, the need to communicate to the legal community at large makes it imperative to write in a manner that reaches a wide audience—attorneys, judges, paralegals, clients, and jurors, to name a few. And the amount of distraction attorneys deal with in their very busy schedules certainly makes reading a laborious task, so making that task easy enough for an 8th grader certainly seems like a logical plan.

You may wonder how the National Center for Educational Statistics determined that the average adult reads on an 8th-grade level. It turns out that studies like the one conducted by the National Center for Educational Statistics have been evolving in the United States for about 90 years. In the beginning, many of the studies focused on assessing texts instead of people. Those stud-

---

1. Irwin Kirsch, *Adult Literacy in America*, http://nces.ed.gov/pubs93/93275.pdf (1993).

ies found that over the history of the written English word, sentences have dramatically shortened in length from an average of about 50 words in Pre-Elizabethan times to 20 words in current usage.[2] Those studies also found that the evolution of written language was to make sentences simpler and more concrete. Not surprisingly, less sophisticated readers need sentences to be simpler and more concrete in order to process what a sentence is trying to convey. Later studies determined that some words are used more frequently than other words in the English language, so younger readers tend to know those more frequently used words while they may not know less frequently used words until they have been reading for many more years.[3]

In the 1950s many researchers began to conduct studies that focused less on the actual text of the documents and more on the reactions of readers themselves to assess reading comprehension. In 1953, a test was developed called "the Cloze test" that could test reader comprehension by deleting words at regular intervals from a sentence and requiring readers to fill those words in.[4] The more words readers can fill in, the better their understanding of the meaning of the sentence. Cloze testing spawned over 1000 studies that looked at varying sentence structures, vocabulary, and style choices.[5] Again, not surprisingly, these tests also found that simple sentences filled with frequently used concrete words are the easiest for readers to comprehend.

In an effort to give some guidance on writing with simple sentences and in simple words, reading comprehension theorists have developed reading difficulty formulas that can be applied to a written passage. One of the most famous is the Flesch-Kincaid Grade Level Test, previously discussed in Chapter 9. This test was developed by a researcher named J. Peter Kincaid who was commissioned by the Department of Defense in the 1970s to develop a standard for writing materials put out for military personnel.[6]

Kincaid used an assessment tool previously developed by Rudolph Flesch in the 1940's that determined the ease with which a reader could read a passage by determining the average words in each sentence in a document and the average amount of syllables in each word. Kincaid tested 531 Navy per-

---

2. William H. Dubay, *The Classic Readability Studies*, http://www.nald.ca/library/research/readab/11.htm.

3. E.B. Fry, J. E. Kress, and D. L. Fountoukidis. The Reading Teacher's Book of Lists. 3d ed. 1993.

4. W. Taylor, "Cloze procedure: A new tool for measuring readability." 30 Journalism quarterly: 415-433 (1953).

5. G.R. Klare, "Readability," 3 Encyclopedia of Educational Research 30:1520–31. (1982).

6. J. Peter Kincaid, *Derivation of New Readability Formulas*, http://www.dtic.mil/dtic/tr/fulltext/u2/a006655.pdf.

sonnel's ability to comprehend 18 passages out of a Navy training manual and to complete a Cloze test on the passages by figuring out what words had been redacted from the passage.

Kincaid was able to use this study to validate the accuracy of Flesch's calculation for the reading difficulty for passages—as the Flesch numbers went up, the Navy personnel's ability to fill in the Cloze blanks and comprehend the passage went down. Additionally, Kincaid was able to assign educational grade levels to the Flesch scale numbers by assessing the passage's difficulty as compared to the educational standards for grade levels at the time. The Flesch-Kincaid Grade Level Test is used today by some of the most popular Word Processing programs to assess the readability of text of passages typed into those programs.

In the 1970s, cognitive theorists began to look at the mental processes behind reading rather than just the text itself to determine what makes writing easy to comprehend.[7] Although these researchers found that different people process reading in different ways, all of these studies supported the previous researchers' findings that simple sentences constructed with concrete and frequently used terminology, increase reader comprehension.[8]

The use of simple language and sentences also seems to have a specialized effect on the reader when the writer is trying to persuade the reader. In the mid-90s, two Canadian psychology researchers looked at the effect of simple language and sentences on the persuasiveness of a message about plea bargaining.[9] To study the effect of language on the persuasiveness of a message, the researchers randomly assigned 104 undergraduate psychology students to one of eight groups that tested how persuaded the students were towards a speaker's argument that involved substantively weak arguments and substantively strong arguments if the arguments were given by a credentialed speaker or an uncredentialed speaker and were explained through complex language and grammatical structures or simple language and simple grammatical structures.

The researchers discovered that when the message was easy to understand, the students were persuaded to be more favorable to plea bargaining than when the arguments where complicated. When the arguments were more compli-

---

7. Nancy Nelson Spivey, *Construing Constructivism: Reading Research in the United States*, http://www.nwp.org/cs/public/download/nwp_file/104/op12.pdf?x-r=pcfile_d.

8. Daniel Felker, *Guidelines for Doc Designers*, http://eric.ed.gov/?id=ED221866, p. 43 (Nov. 1981).

9. Carolyn L. Hafer, Kelly L. Reynolds, and Monica A. Obertynsky, MESSAGE COMPREHENSIBILITY AND PERSUASION: EFFECTS OF COMPLEX LANGUAGE IN COUNTERATTITUDINAL APPEALS TO LAYPEOPLE, Social Cognition, Vol. 14, No.4, pp. 317–37 (1996).

cated, the students were persuaded by the arguments of the more credentialed speakers more than the less credentialed speaker. The researchers hypothesized that this was because the students were relying on the credibility of the speaker to determine if the arguments were believable. The researchers also noted that the students seemed to remember more of the speaker's arguments when listening to the speaker who used the more accessible language. This study seems to indicate that unless a writer has a particularly strong reputation as an expert in the subject matter, the best method for communicating a persuasive message is through simple language and grammatical structures.

Looking at these studies, the advice that many legal writing textbooks give to new legal writers to write in simple prose and to use short, concise sentences that use a simple grammatical structure appears to be supported by a long history of readability research. Perhaps the most striking study regarding the simplicity of writing and its effect on readers is the study on persuasion. For those writers who believe that writing in lofty words and with complex sentences sends a signal to a reader that the writer is intelligent and believable, those traits appear to lessen the persuasive effect. It follows that for the average legal writer, who may not be known as a credible expert in the particular subject matter of the document, readers will comprehend the document easier and be more persuaded by arguments that are written in an easy-to-read format.

Take a look at these two sentences. Which one do you find more persuasive?

Sentence 1:

Weiderman was not held for too long because he was released immediately after the necklace was found.

Sentence 2:

The length of the detention of the alleged-shoplifter Weiderman was not too lengthy because as soon as the manager became aware that the good was recovered, Weiderman was released by the store employee.

PART V
Improving Your Legal Writing

Chapter 18

Learning Legal Writing

The gold standard for legal writing instruction is similar to writing instruction in other disciplines—students are taught some general guidelines for how to write particularized documents by teachers or by reading textbooks, students then attempt to write a similar document, the teacher gives feedback on that attempt, the student rewrites the documents based on that feedback, and then receives feedback from the teacher on the rewrite. But you may be wondering what you can do outside of a structured class environment to assess your writing and improve it. It turns out that bettering your legal writing skills is best accomplished by having a mental awareness of the limitations of the science that we know about reading and accepting that opinions on writing mimic opinions on art—the beauty of a particular document, just like a piece of art, is subjective.

First and foremost, writing students need to accept that writing improvement is a slow process. Researchers have determined that gains in writing strengths may be slow and methodical and not at all as drastic as students may believe they are from their structured writing classes. A study conducted on 80 undergraduate psychology students found that when students followed this learn-write-feedback-rewrite-feedback model to learn how to write introductions to academic papers, their grades did improve, on average, when their writing was assessed by the teacher that gave them feedback on the first writing attempt.[1] But this correlation was not as strong when the paper was independently assessed by a "blind" grader who was equally as credentialed as the teacher to assess the paper. The "blind" grader used the same rubric as the teacher who gave feedback, but unlike the teacher who gave the original feedback, the "blind" grader did not know when he or she was reading a first or a second draft.

While 82% of the student papers graded by the teacher who gave the feedback received higher grades, only 57% of the papers did when assessed by

---

1. Mark A. Stellmack, *Review, Revise, and Resubmit: The Effects of Self-Critique, Peer Review, and Instructor Feedback on Student Writing*, 39 Teaching of Psychology 235 (2012).

"blind" graders. Clearly, the grades from the original teachers who gave feedback on the first draft had some sort of bias. The researchers hypothesized that the bias may be the desire to reward the students for working hard on their papers or for making the specific changes the feedback teacher had requested. The researchers also indicated that the students may just have become more adept at writing for the subjective preferences of the teacher, but may not have been making strides in their writing on a more objective level. Whatever the reason, it appears that improvement in writing comes slowly—even in a class devoted to the study of writing, students only had a 50% chance of their rewrite being better than their original document.

In an article based on anecdotal observations of six second semester law students, a legal writing teacher found that the biggest predictors of a successful grade improvement between the first semester writing grade and second semester writing grade were: 1) a larger amount of time spent writing and planning the writing as compared to other students, 2) a larger amount of time spent speaking to the professor outside of class, and 3) more note-taking on the teacher's lectures and readings in the course textbook.[2] But one of the most striking differences the teacher found between the students who improved their grade the next semester and those that didn't, was the ability of some students to use the negative feedback received on their first semester paper as a point of motivation, instead of a point of frustration.

It seems that the students who became frustrated, blamed the teacher, and failed to take responsibility for their first semester grade and seek out ways to improve their second semester grade, did not improve their grade like the students did who doggedly pursued improving their skills in the second semester through an increased focus and dedication to learning the attributes of good writing. While not statistically sound, this article does seem to describe what we know from the empirical data—writing is inherently subjective.

Although there are some things we know about good writing from empirical data, those writing choices may not be the best way to communicate for a particularized individual in absolutely every writing scenario. For example, the empirical data showing that organization helps reader comprehension, and clear and concise prose is easier for readers to process than complicated and dense prose supports two conflicting choices of how to write a document in an effective manner. You may remember from the chapter on narrative that choosing to use a narrative approach to explain an area of the law where it is unclear

---

2. Anne Enquist, Unlocking the Secrets of Highly Successful Legal Writing Students, 82 St. John's L.R. 609 (208).

how a rule applies can be a choice that is extremely effective when a clear cause-and-effect relationship can be established for the reader. However, a similarly effective explanation can be written by simply explaining the syllogistic reasoning behind the rules and explaining how that syllogistic reasoning ends with a rule that has no clear application to the facts at hand. If drafted correctly, both paths can clearly and effectively communicate the point to the reader. So the best path is largely a piece of art—a call on what will be most subjectively likeable for the audience of the document.

Although bettering your writing skills is a slow and incremental process that can include some uncertainty regarding the choices a writer should make in a particular writing situation, those choices may be more confidently made the more information writers have at their disposal. Empirical studies, like the ones discussed in this book, or the advice of writing teachers who use empirical studies can give solid direction on many writing decisions. However, in the absence of an empirical study, the next best thing seems to be a writer reviewing a peer's writing or having that peer review their writing. Because this is something anyone can do outside of the legal writing classroom, peer modeling and peer evaluation are valuable tools for writers who want to continue bettering their writing.

Peer modeling occurs when a writer trying to make writing decisions about a particular document reads a similar document written by another writer. In a study conducted on undergraduate students in Holland, researchers determined that students wrote a better analysis of scientific studies if they first observed other students completing the same task.[3] A later study determined that students must be looking at peer writing that is better than theirs to have any appreciable benefit to their own writing.[4]

Peer review occurs when a writer seeks out a review of a document by another writer. Like peer modeling, peer review has also been shown to be an effective way for writers to better their writing. In one study that conducted a meta-analysis of over 60 studies that have looked at the value of peer reviews, it was determined that peer comments on a draft of a document produced 50% better revisions than a teacher's review of the same paper.[5]

---

3. M. Raedts, G. Rijlaarsdam, L. Van Waes, & F. Daems, (2007). *Observational learning through video-based models: Impact on students' accuracy of self-efficacy beliefs, task knowledge and writing performances.* British Journal of Educational Psychology (2011).

4. Braaksma, M. A. H., Rijlaarsdam, G., & Van den Bergh, H., (2002). Observational Learning and the Effects of Model-Observer Similarity. Journal of Educational Psychology, 94(2), 405–415.

5. George Hillocks, Jr., *What Works in Teaching Composition: A Meta-Analysis of Experimental Treatment Studies*, 93 Am. J. of Educ. 133–170 (1984).

Because writing is a slow process, it is not one that is mastered in one se-mester of law school or, perhaps, in the entirety of law school. Indeed, one recent survey of lawyers and judges indicated that 57% of respondents thought recent law graduates did not write well.[6] This indicates that writing well may be a lifelong process for many attorneys. Because of the length of this process, it is critical that writers, new or old, have tools at their disposal to evaluate and improve their writing. Luckily, most attorney work environments provide easy access to peer writers, which should offer an unlimited supply of useful feedback for writers looking to improve their writing.

So even in those situations where writing decisions may not be clear based on the empirical knowledge that we have regarding readers of legal documents, deciding the finer points of the "art" of legal writing may be better determined through having peers review your writing or looking at similar writing of your peers.

---

6. Susan Hanley Kosse and David T. ButleRitchie, *How Judges, Teachers, and Legal Writing Teachers Assess the Writing Skills of New Graduates: a Comparative Study*, 53 J. Legal Educ. 80 (2003).

PART VI
Science and the Ethics
of Legal Writing

Chapter 19

Are Bad Writers Bad Lawyers?

No, it's unlikely. There are probably thousands of good lawyers that are bad writers. But if the word "bad" is taken to mean "incompetent"[1] when it modifies "writer" and "evil,"[2] when it modifies "lawyer," is it still false? Are poor or sloppy legal writers more likely to be formally disciplined by a state bar for ethical misconduct?

"I doubt that anyone in this class will intentionally or willfully violate the lawyer's code of professional conduct." Many law professors say something similar to 1L legal writing students in one of the first classes of the first semester of law school. We, however, then add, "if you do violate an ethical rule, it will almost certainly be due to incompetence or carelessness." And, for the coup de grace, finish with "and the first place this carelessness will manifest itself is in your legal writing."

You may have heard the news story about attorneys in California who may have cost their client one million dollars when they failed to timely file a request for attorney fees.[3] With respect to carelessness in legal writing itself, you have probably heard the story about the million-dollar comma, in which the U.S. government was deprived of $1 million in revenue because a misplaced comma allowed fruit importers to claim they were exempt from taxation, and other horror stories of attorneys who were humiliated by their failure to adequately edit or proofread a document.

The same critique can be made about incompetent legal research. The failure of the entire United States justice system (and the attorneys who filed ten briefs in the case) to identify a 2008 military statute that provided the death penalty for child rape, resulted in Justice Anthony Kennedy wrongly concluding that

---

1. http://www.merriam-webster.com/dictionary/bad.

2. *Id.*

3. Peter Lattman, *A Litigator's Nightmare: Late Filing Costs Client $1 Million*, Wall Street Journal (Jan. 8, 2008).

"capital punishment for child rape was contrary to the 'evolving standards of decency' by which the court judges how the death penalty is applied."[4] In fact, the military had such a statute currently on its books and thus capital punishment was not contrary to those standards.

While it is probably not surprising that attorneys who are careless may be subject to formal discipline, the anecdotal evidence hardly shows a correlation between carelessness and discipline, much less between careless writing and discipline. In fact, several studies have isolated the profile of attorneys most likely to be disciplined.[5] According to the Illinois Annual Report of the Attorney Registration and Disciplinary Commission for 2011, attorneys most likely to receive bar discipline are older, male attorneys who are solo practitioners and suffer from depression or alcoholism.[6]

Until recently, however, there has been no empirical evidence that our warning was anything more than another untested aphorism that law professors glibly disseminate to students as a matter of course during the first year of law school. That all changed when Professors Long and Christensen decided to compare memos and briefs written and submitted to a court from two groups: attorneys that had been disciplined and attorneys that had not been disciplined.[7] All of the briefs and memoranda analyzed had been published by Westlaw. They analyzed the briefs from both groups for "careless" writing errors such as subject-verb agreement, pronoun-antecedent agreement, that v. which, phrasal adjectives, its v. it's, commas, semicolons, your v. you're, affect v. effect, then v. than, since v. because, fewer v. less, over v. more than, amount v. number, typos, and misspellings.[8]

While a complete study has not yet been published, a preliminary study of Florida attorneys showed that there was, in fact, a statistically significant difference. Such a difference was expected, but what was unexpected was the extent of the difference in the error rate between the two groups. When considering punctuation errors, word choice errors, and typos together, the error rate of

---

4. Linda Greenhouse, *In Court Ruling on Executions, a Factual Flaw,* New York Times (July 2, 2008).

5. *See e.g.* Illinois annual report of the Attorney Registration and Disciplinary Commission for 2011, www.iatdc.org/AnnualReport2011.pdf and Debra Moss Curtis and Billie Jo Kaufman, A Public View of Attorney Discipline in Florida: Statistics, Commentary and Analysis of Disciplinary Actions Against Licensed Attorneys in the State of Florida from 1988–2002, 28 Nova L. Rev 669 (2004).

6. *Id.*

7. Lance N. Long and William F. Christensen, *Are Bad Writers Bad Lawyers? A Statistical Analysis of Disciplined and Non-Disciplined Attorney Writing Errors* (2014) (Unpublished data and manuscript in the possession of the authors).

8. *Id.*

the disciplined attorneys was more than 50% higher than that of the non-disciplined attorneys. While the disciplined attorneys averaged 3.5 errors per 100 words, the non-disciplined attorneys averaged only 2.3 errors per 100 words. Statistically comparing the two groups with a Wilcoxon Rank Sum test, the difference between the two groups had a p-value of 0.002.[9]

The difference in writing was so noticeable that, after a while, Long and Christensen's research assistants were able to accurately guess whether a given memo or brief was written by a disciplined or a non-disciplined attorney without knowing the attorney's discipline status. Of course, the results do not show any causal relationship between an attorney's careless writing errors and unethical conduct, but the correlation appears to be fairly solid; attorneys who make more careless writing errors in memos and briefs submitted to a court are more likely to face formal attorney discipline.

Legal writing professors tell students that sloppy legal writing should be a big red flag that ethical misconduct and formal attorney discipline may be looming in the future. What can you do? Pay attention to the signs that you are inadvertently being incompetent or unethical: attacking the other side or the judge instead of the law, not addressing "gaps" in the argument, not checking sources or citations, waiting until the last minute to draft, or not revising work product. Any of these actions should cause a law student, or a lawyer, to consider the possibility that similar sloppiness may exist in other aspects of one's practice, which may lead to formal discipline.

---

9. *Id.*

PART VII
Science and Legal Writing Top Ten

Chapter 20

The Top Ten Takeaways from *The Science Behind the Art of Legal Writing*

"For this reason, a private-language, in which 'individual words ... are to refer to what can only be known to the person speaking; to his immediate private sensations ...' is not a genuine, meaningful, rule-governed language. The signs in language can only function when there is a possibility of judging the correctness of their use, 'so the use of [a] word stands in need of a justification which everybody understands.'"[1]

Ludwig Wittgenstein

What can a legal writer do to have the best probability of having her legal memorandum or brief understood and its reasoning accepted? The preceding chapters have discussed different issues and the science behind them. This chapter provides a quick review, in a "top ten" format, of the most important practices that research indicates will foster reader comprehension and persuasion. Arguably, but not certainly, starting from the most to the least important, here are ten practices a legal writer can utilize to ensure that the reader understands and will more likely be persuaded by an argument:

---

1. Biletzki, Anat and Matar, Anat, "Ludwig Wittgenstein," The Stanford Encyclopedia of Philosophy (Spring 2014 Edition), Edward N. Zalta (ed.), http://plato.stanford.edu/archives/spr2014/entries/wittgenstein/.

Top Ten Takeaways from *The Science Behind the Art of Legal Writing*

1. Write for your audience.

Some interesting studies have demonstrated that no matter how objective a reader tries to be in his or her assessment of a written piece, everyone has subjective preferences that are impossible to avoid. The single most important thing any writer can do is try to figure out what those subjective preferences are.

2. Write concisely and clearly.

The empirical research indicates that a reader is more persuaded by an argument that is easier to comprehend. For all readers, including highly educated readers, it is generally easier to read shorter sentences and shorter words. More simplistic word choice and structure allow the message to be communicated more clearly, as it is not buried in complex sentences and lofty language.

3. Use outlining, but outlining can happen before or after a document is written.

We know that written pieces are consistently assessed as qualitatively better when the writing is outlined. However, that outlining can happen before an author begins writing or it can happen after the writing is underway in a process many refer to as "reverse outlining." Because anxious writers can grow more anxious when forced to outline ahead of time, it actually appears to be a more efficient use of an anxious writer's time to outline after the majority of the piece is written.

4. Organize paragraphs with topic sentences.

Studies by cognitive psychologists have shown readers comprehend information better and retain it longer if the information is explained in paragraphs beginning with topic sentences that state the goal of that paragraph. This allows the reader to more easily comprehend the rest of the information in a paragraph.

5. *Use introductory and transitional phrases.*

Studies from the field of educational instruction have determined that reader comprehension increases when instruction begins with broad overviews of the details that will be forthcoming and when connections are made between the details for the learner. These studies suggest that introductions and transitions are key to increasing the comprehension of complex subjects for readers of legal writing.

6. *Explain the law before applying it.*

Cognitive psychology studies show that the best structure for comprehension is organizing sentences in a sequential order that allows each new sentence to refer to some information that was covered in a proceeding sentence. Explaining the law before the law is applied to the facts helps readers with the step-by-step processing of information. By explaining the law first, the reader can refer back to the law and more easily comprehend how the law relates to the new set of facts.

7. *Include emotional reasoning.*

Recent cognitive psychology theory suggests writing that appeals to values or emotions is actually the argument that persuades and logical reasoning is simply a mechanism the brain uses to justify its previous decision based on emotion. Although logical reasoning is important in legal arguments, a writer's persuasiveness can be enhanced when logical arguments are balanced with appeals to the reader's emotions.

8. *Incorporate narrative.*

We know from psychology studies that writing in a storytelling style pulls the reader into the written word better than other possible styles of writing. Increasing the reader's attention in this manner will benefit the reader's comprehension of the writer's message. Additionally, a storytelling style written correctly also gives the reader the satisfaction of connecting pieces of a story into a cause-and-effect relationship. This sense of satisfaction for a reader makes statements written in a narrative style particularly persuasive.

9. Think about formatting.

While often taken for granted, fonts play an important role in conveying words. When formatting your document, think about who will be reading it and how they will likely be reading it. Then choose a font that will ease the readability of your document for that particular reader. When in doubt, research has shown that the font Baskerville is 1.5% more persuasive than any other font. However, before becoming too creative, it is important to make sure you follow any guidelines given by the court so as not to have your submission discarded, rejected, or overlooked (or overly scrutinized); failure to follow these guidelines would negate any hope for persuasive benefit.

10. Edit carefully.

Ample evidence exists to show that even though there is less concern about technical grammar usage today as compared with thirty or even ten years ago, there is still enough concern about it to err on the side of knowing and using conventional grammar. Before submitting any kind of legal document, be sure to carefully proofread in order to avoid any glaring errors that may hinder the persuasive power of your argument.

Index